Through Her Eyes:
A Man's Guide to His Wife's Need for Romance

By

Rev. R. David Morrow, LMFT

Fruitful Vine Family Ministries

Vanceboro, NC

First Printing: 2017
Edited by Janie Taylor, Ph.D., LMFT
Photographer: Amanda R. Morrow
Interior Design: Jerry Goff

Library of Congress Cataloging-in-Publication Data
Morrow, R. David
Through Her Eyes: A Man's Guide to his Wife's Need for Romance
ISBN: 9780692944585
1. Marriage 2. Self-help

For permissions, or sales:

David Morrow
Fruitful Vine Family Ministries LLC
Vanceboro, NC 28586

DavidMorrowLMFT@gmail.com

www.romancingyourwife.com

Dedication

Peter Kuzmic said "Hope is the ability to hear the music of the future... Faith is having the courage to dance to it today." This book is dedicated to all of the individuals, couples, and families who have sat with me and vulnerably shared their life struggles. It is my hope that each of you learned something from our conversations that you can use to improve your life. I have learned and grown personally and professionally from each of you, and for that I am very grateful. It is my prayer that each of you can look toward the future and faithfully dance.

Acknowledgements

I must acknowledge a number of people because, without their influence, investment, and encouragement in my life, it is very unlikely that this book would ever have been written. First, I want to express appreciation to my wife. Cheryl, you have listened to my crazy ideas and help me sort the good stuff from the junk. You have accepted me completely and loved me in ways I have never deserved. You have shared your beautiful soul with me, and been an essential part of helping me find peace. Loving you and sharing life with you is my true joy.

I want to say thank you to my children, Stephen and Amanda Morrow. When I think about your growing up years, it is easy to focus on the ways I should have done things differently. Now that both of you have transitioned into adulthood, I see the trajectory of your paths, and I believe that you will follow God's plan for you in a way that will bring peace and joy to you. I am so looking forward to watching and enjoying all of your successes.

I want to express my gratitude to my step-daughters, Caitlyn and Caroline Sutton. Blending a family is not easy. You have accepted me into your home without real struggle or difficulty. In the same way that I am looking forward to watching and enjoying Stephen and Amanda's successes, I likewise want to be loving and supportive for all you want to accomplish. Additionally, I want to acknowledge my mother and father-in-law who have embraced me into the family with love, grace, and affirmation.

I want to thank Dr. Janie Taylor. As my supervisor, you have been more affirming of me and my work than any other person with whom I have shared the privilege of working. It was your endorsement that really moved me from a bunch of ideas in my head to sitting down and starting to type. I am so thankful for you and the wonderful company for whom we both work. CareNet Inc., and Wake Forest Baptist

Health empower us to chase our dreams, and that is worth more than gold. As my editor, your gracious expertise is something I will always cherish.

Words can't describe the positive influence that my Mom and Dad had on me. My sister Connie and I grew up in an environment where we learned the value of work, the joy of laughter, and the meaning of family. Mom and Dad's examples were valuable models to follow. I was able to observe their matrimonial bond through the joys and struggles of life, and even though Dad is enjoying the Lord's retirement plan in heaven, the bond Mom shares with him continues. As Mom states, she and Dad are both "still in God's world. We are just in different rooms now." I look forward to the day that the four of us can gather around a piano and again sing praises to our Lord in four-part harmony.

Finally, to God the Father, God the Son, and God the Holy Spirit, I give you thanks. I give you praise. I give you my heart, my soul, and my life. I praise you for your unconditional love. I praise you for your amazing grace. I praise you for your loving guidance. You are the God of Restoration. You brought restoration to me. Thank you.

Foreword

"The fear of the Lord is instruction in wisdom, and humility goes before honor" (Proverbs 15:33, NRSV). There's something wonderful about a man who has wrestled with real life, made his share of mistakes, mustered the courage and humility to analyze them and learn from them, and then with candor and grace shares his lessons and observations with others. What a gift! In "Through Her Eyes" David will teach you what your wife needs, why she needs it, and how you can pull it off. He uses short and to-the-point biblically based guidance that will give you confidence in your romantic creativity. You will not be disappointed!

Rev. W. Chris Jenkins
Executive Pastor
Hope Restorations
www.hoperestorationsnc.org

TABLE OF CONTENTS

Introduction

Men, it's time for a huddle. Imagine a football team that never has a huddle. They always try to predict what the other team members will do without communicating. The offensive line does not know if they should create a pocket for the quarterback or try to create a hole for the running back. If the quarterback decides to pass, he does not know exactly where the pass receivers are going. So, it takes extra seconds for him to observe their route. Those few seconds are all a defensive linebacker needs to run through the hole the offensive linemen created for their own running back to carry the ball. The linebacker plows into the quarterback full speed ahead with the force of a freight train. The quarterback very slowly stands to his feet, as the linebacker dances in celebration, and the hometown crowd moans in frustration and disbelief.

Luckily, you only have one wife, as opposed to ten teammates on the field. You don't have anyone actively opposing your marital success, and you don't have an audience that gives positive or negative self-serving feedback for the entire world to hear. However, many husbands try "to do" romance in their marriage without a huddle. Men do not take the time to learn about his wife's need for romance. So, when his bride expresses her frustration, he will often inquire through exasperation, "Just tell me what to do and I will do it." Ladies often respond with something like this, "If I have to tell you what to do, then it is not romantic. That doesn't count." So, what is a guy to do? Guys often do nothing, and then get blindsided by their wife's unhappiness (similar to the scenario of the above-mentioned quarterback.)

If we can huddle together now, then you might avoid getting sacked! For the last 26 years, I have worked fulltime in the mental health field. Since 2008, I have worked both in private practice and in an agency setting as a licensed marriage and family therapist. I have shared thousands of conversations with individuals, couples, and families that were focused on solving a problem, relieving the symptoms of a mental illness, increasing marital intimacy, assisting couples to survive the destruction of infidelity, helping individuals quit smoking or lose weight with hypnosis, and a whole host of other issues. Generally, I am very successful at helping my clients improve their lives. The thing I enjoy doing the most is working with couples. Therefore, during that process, I have spent many hours listening to ladies complain about what their husbands will not do. I want to share the nuggets of wisdom I have developed about romance with you in a way that will not make you feel like you are being forced to watch a chick flick on the Hallmark Channel.

I am going to speak to you, man to man, about romance, and how the things you did during the time you dated your wife will not work the same way now that you are married. I will help you understand why your wife needs you to do something, but she can't tell you what it is. I will help you determine ways to do those things she needs, and I will help you do it in a way that is fun without making you feel like you have lost your "man card." The ideas presented in this text are generally applicable to all people in the American and similar cultures. However, in addition to being a licensed marriage and family therapist, I am also an ordained minister in the Christian faith. So, I will share with you the biblical and spiritual guidelines that back up my assertions.

For now, just remember this: *"As a husband, it is your job to do everything in your power to create an environment in which your wife can grow and become all God created her to be."*[1] This is a statement I repeatedly heard quoted by Dr. Leigh Conver, who was one of my seminary professors at Southern Baptist Theological Seminary in Louisville Kentucky. He was quoting Dr. Andrew Lester, a retired pastoral counseling professor. Creating that environment is the essence of romance. If you struggle to create a positive affirming environment for your wife, then she will most likely view your efforts at romance as Jesus described the Pharisees: "Whitewashed Tombs – beautiful on the outside but filled on the inside with dead people's bones and all sorts of impurity."[2] You will discover that romance is not something that you do on special occasions. It is the daily investment of yourself into the lady God created for you. This daily investment of you trying to see the world through her eyes - and then taking steps to make that world a more enjoyable place for her to live - is the essence of romance.

At the end of each chapter, I will share a written prayer with you and invite you to use that prayer as a point of meditation for the day. The point of this meditation is for you to explore ideas and discover ways that you can personally apply the information in that chapter.

I know you don't have a lot of time, and you probably do not enjoy reading a book like this. So, I will keep the chapters short enough that you can read a chapter during the time it takes to sit on your throne. I feel reasonably sure you love your wife. If you didn't, you would not take the time to read this. So, join me on a journey to explore behaviors that will meet your wife's needs for romance in ways that give you joy, peace, and satisfaction.

Prayer: LORD, help me to learn to love my wife with the same unconditional love that you give to me. Help me to discover her real wants, needs, and desires. Give me the courage to meet those wants, needs, and desires in a way that will be pleasing to her, and bring you glory, honor, and praise. Amen.

Part 1: What is Romance . . . Really?

Chapter 1

Defining "Romance"

L et's be real: Most men see romance as a tool to convince his wife to have sex. In fact, most every man is happy and content if he has money in his pocket, and is having sex as often as he determines is reasonable. As men, we must understand that there are more differences between us and our wives than just biology. Their view of sex is different. (Of course, there are exceptions to nearly every rule.) Their view of romance is different. Their view of quality entertainment is different. Their view of parenting is different. Their view of the future is different.

To illustrate this point, allow me to share a story with you: I once facilitated a marriage enrichment seminar for a church. There were approximately 25 couples and the range of time the couples had been married varied widely. There was one couple that had been married a few months. There was another couple that had been married 67 years. One of the activities I facilitated involved a discussion about sex. I split the people into two groups based on their gender. I had a dry-erase board and I drew a line down the middle of it so I could record the answers from each group. I asked each group to have a private discussion in which they would identify specific words that applied to sex. Each group came back to the discussion with a list of approximately 20 words or phrases. The thing that was so interesting is that the only word that was on both lists was the word "fun." Both genders, in that group, consider sex fun. Yet, they thought it was fun for completely different reasons!

There is a portion of romance that is sexual; but if that is your primary focus, then you will fail at meeting your wife's need for romance. She sees it in a completely different way. In order to meet her need, and not just use her to meet your need, then you must learn to look at romance *through her eyes.*

So, if romance is not about getting sex, then what is it? I am sure you have heard the old adage, "It's the thought that counts." When it comes to romance, through your lady's eyes, this statement is exactly true. When you and your wife were dating, you chased her. You expressed your interest in her. In essence, you tried to convince her that you were a person in which she could wisely invest her life. One of the differences between men and women is this: When you both say, "I Do," ladies, more often than men, need for that chase to continue after the wedding. She needs you to communicate, on a regular basis, that you still chose her. *Romance is using your own creativity to express the love that you feel in your heart in ways that make her feel loved, honored, and cherished.* We will explore more about the practical application of that in the chapters that follow.

Prayer: *LORD, I need your help in learning to love my wife romantically. Her needs are not like mine. Help me to see through her eyes so I can improve our relationship with each other and ultimately be closer to you as individuals and as a couple. Amen.*

Chapter 2

So, How Do You Do It?

Far too often, men think of romance as picking up the required anniversary card, chocolates, and flowers once a year. Remember: *It's the thought that counts.* If you don't put any thought in it, for her it will not count. This is why you must use your own creativity to express the love that is in your heart. Now, don't lose your mind by telling yourself how you are not creative. I am not talking about softly finger-picking a guitar by candle light while quoting a love sonnet that you wrote for her. *When you say to yourself, and to your wife, that you are not creative enough to do this, she will hear you say that she is not important enough for you to put forth some effort and try.*

Remember when you were a kid and you brought home some type of art project from school. You shared it with your mom or grandmother, and she just loved it. She told you how good it was. Now, you know that it was not the greatest piece of artwork she had ever seen. It was not the artwork that was exciting to her. It was the fact that you chose to make it for her and then give it to her.

Your wife is the same way. She wants to know that she remains in your heart. That is why she can't tell you what to do to be romantic. In order for her to feel that she is still in your heart, the expression must be initiated by you, and come from your heart. She likes unexpected surprises that communicate that you are trying to see the world through her eyes. She likes seeing you try to understand what it is like for her now that she has invested her life into partnership with you. She likes seeing you understanding her world and doing something to positively impact it. This is why romance is not just about taking dance lessons so you can learn to recreate "the lift" from her favorite movie "Dirty Dancing."[1] You will lift her spirit by simply asking yourself this question: What is my bride's life like today, and how can I join her to make it a little easier? The more you work together to share the joys and struggles of life, the

15

more you will have an increasing number of things to celebrate. In the next chapters, I will give you concrete examples of how to see opportunities for romance, and then prompt you to take action. Of course, it is not your job to depend on me for suggestions. Creativity is a skill. Develop yours.

Prayer: *LORD, Help me to learn to see opportunities for romance. Help me to develop my creativity. Help me to have the courage to act on my creative ideas. Amen.*

Chapter 3

Spiritually Motivating Your Creativity

So, how do you keep yourself motivated to be romantic? In the introduction, I referenced a quote which originated with Dr. Andrew Lester: "*As a husband, it is your job to do everything in your power to create an environment in which your wife can grow and become all God created her to be.*" To illustrate this scripturally, let's look at Psalms 128. This short psalm highlights a picture of the family.

Psalm 128

A song of ascents.

¹ Blessed are all who fear the LORD,
   who walk in obedience to him.
² You will eat the fruit of your labor;
   blessings and prosperity will be yours.
³ Your wife will be like a fruitful vine
   within your house;
your children will be like olive shoots
   around your table.
⁴ Yes, this will be the blessing
   for the man who fears the LORD.

⁵ May the LORD bless you from Zion;
   may you see the prosperity of Jerusalem
   all the days of your life.
⁶ May you live to see your children's children—
   peace be on Israel.

Imagine yourself for a moment as a farmer who is listening to these words for the first time. You have been taught all of your life about the ways of God. You have heard the stories of Abraham, Isaac, Jacob, Moses, Joshua, and others. You recognize that walking in the ways of LORD is in your own best interest. You have enjoyed some times where your crops have been plentiful. All of that seems great.

Then, you hear that your wife is like a fruitful vine *within your house*. You know that a fruitful vine growing there is a tremendous resource. As a farmer, you also know that you must provide that fruitful vine the environment that it needs. You can't (or shouldn't) just treat that vine like any other vine. You have to investigate and specifically know the needs of your vine, which may be different from another vine. You must provide the right amount of water and fertilizer, and ensure that it has good sunlight. Otherwise, it will stop producing fruit. It then occurs to you that if your wife is like that, then you must do what you can to provide the right environment for her to become all God created her to be. You can be assured that if you do your part in providing that environment, then most likely your vine will continue to produce fruit. By providing the environment that your spouse needs, she will most likely produce the environment that meets your needs.

You also know that olive trees will live about 500 years and then the tree above ground will die, but the root system will not. Around the base of the trunk, olive shoots begin to sprout. Once the dead part of the tree has been cut down, these olive shoots will become the new branches. Therefore, your olive shoots that are around your table will help your family "live forever."

As you focus on the behaviors you want to change, remember the "ways of the LORD" bring peace. "Family" is where the sense of self and happiness begins. Be satisfied with what you can do with your hands. Don't look outside yourself for the sense of who you are. Providing that your family is not abusive, recognize the peace that comes from family being together, and let it "be well with you."

Prayer: LORD, *help me to pay attention to the environment that I provide for my wife and my children. It is my job to explore and determine their needs, and do all I can to meet them. I need to do this regardless of what they do for me. As a spiritual leader in my home, it is my job to set the example. Fill me with your love for my wife and children. Help me to express your love in ways that bring peace and joy to all who live in my home. Amen.*

Chapter 4

Identify the Needs of Her Environment

It is all about the environment. However, if you don't know what your wife needs in her environment, then you have just confirmed for yourself that you are not consistently meeting your wife's needs for romance. It is time to make some changes . . . serious changes.

If you are completely clueless about your next step, here is a great place to start. Dr. Gary Chapman, who is the senior associate pastor at Calvary Baptist Church in Winston-Salem, NC, and has led marriage enrichment weekend seminars for years, published a book in 1992 titled The Five Love Langauges: The Secret to Love That Lasts.[1] This book has sold more than 10 million copies, and a revised edition came out in 2015. Dr. Chapman's basic idea is that people give and receive love in five different ways. These types of expressing love (love languages if you will) are very different from each other. Most individuals will identify with one primary love language and one secondary love language.

Let's pretend for a moment that your wife's native language is English. She also took some Spanish in high school, but has not "used it" very much since graduation. If you said "I love you" to her, she would obviously understand. She might also get it if you said "Te Amo" (Spanish). However, if you said "ich liebe dich" (German), "jag älskar dig" (Swedish) or "je t'aime" (French), she would not understand. As valuable as your love for her is, she can experience it as useless as counterfeit money if it is not expressed (spoken) in the right language.

Dr. Chapman's five love languages include quality time, acts of service, physical touch, receiving gifts, and words of affirmation. There is not anything bad on this list, but in order to customize your expressions of love to your particular "fruitful vine", you must know how she will best receive (hear) it.

I will have more to say about these five love languages and the practical application of them in the coming chapters. For now, go to www.5lovelanguages.com. There is a free assessment that you and your wife can take which will reveal your respective love languages. This assessment is available online, or it can be printed as a pdf. The assessment has 30 statements, and each statement begins with "It's more meaningful to me when . . ." Following this beginning of the sentence, there are two different completions of the sentence. The person taking the assessment must then choose which of the two completions of the sentence is most personally accurate. It takes less than 5 minutes (10 at max) to take the assessment and score it, even if you use the pdf and do the scoring manually.

Dr. Chapman asserts that individuals who do not purposefully identify the love language of their spouse and seek to express love in that language, will express love to their spouse in their own love language by default.[2] As an extreme example, I had a co-worker that wanted to start a lawn-care business. So, he gave his wife a commercial grade lawn mower as an anniversary present! This is not the type of mistake you want to make or continue making. The act of asking your wife to take this assessment is in itself romantic because it expresses your desire to learn more about her needs, wants, and desires. Without that information, you are shooting in the dark. Zig Ziglar said, "If you aim at nothing, you'll hit it every time."[3] Expressing love to your wife is something that requires your time, effort, and attention in order to hit the bulls eye.

We are near the end of part 1. In part 2, I will give you 23 practical applications of "romance." My hope is that you will take these applications and apply your own creativity to them, based on your wife's individual needs. This will enable you to meet your "fruitful vine's" needs, and she in turn will hopefully produce fruit in a way that she can enjoy meeting yours.

Prayer: *LORD, Help me to recognize that my wife may receive love in ways that are different from the way I automatically give love. Help me to easily see ways to meet her need of being loved. As always, help me to be a conduit of your unconditional love to my fruitful vine. Help me to see her as you see her and love her as you love her. Amen.*

Part 2: Practical Applications

Chapter 5

"Sweep" Her off Her Feet

According to the United States Department of Labor's Bureau of Labor Statistics, men between the ages of 25 and 65 provide an average of 17.2 hours of unpaid household work each week. Ladies between the ages of 25 and 65, on the other hand, provide an average of 29.4 hours of unpaid household work per week. Therefore, there is a 12.2 hours difference in the household work that is provided by ladies as compared to that done by men. To be fair, men work an average of 3 hours more per week outside of the home in paid work than ladies. Yet, the ladies 29.4 hours added to the men's 17.2 hours reveals that it takes an average of 46.6 hours per week to run a household.[1]

Of course, every family should function in whatever way is best for it. Here is my point: If you do not play an active role in planning and sharing your household responsibilities, and just dump all or part of them on your wife, she is not going to feel positively about her life investment in you. With most households requiring two incomes to support it, you can't reasonably expect your wife to work 12 more hours than you do and still be happy about it.

Take a moment to look at these categories:

- Food and drink preparation
- Cleaning
- Laundry
- Household management
- Lawn and garden
- Maintenance and repair
- Caring for household members (like children)
- Purchasing goods and services
- Traveling (to the grocery store or a child's activities)

Do the math. What percentage of these household responsibilities do you do? What percentage does your wife do? Is the division of labor reasonably fair (based on the working outside of the home scenario) in your family? Are you assisting your wife by requiring that your children participate in the household responsibilities? Have you prompted your children about the necessity of doing these tasks in a timely manner? By trying to see all of these types of things through her eyes, and then taking action on them, she will experience a feeling of connectedness and partnership with you. This is required for her to feel loved, honored, and cherished.

Let's assume for a moment that the division of labor at your house is accepted by everyone and everyone is satisfied with it. We must be realistic and acknowledge that your house is not going to always be clean. Food preparation is not always going to go smoothly, and the laundry is not always going to be caught up. Life happens. Here is an opportunity for you to be romantic!

When I am working professionally with couples, I often hear ladies complain that their husbands will not do anything around the house. Don't wait for her to ask you or even tell you to do something. *Initiative is romantic (at least through your wife's lenses).* This is especially true if your wife's primary love language is acts of service. Look around and see something that needs to be done. This does not have to be a big project like cleaning out the attic or garage. Guys generally do not care as much about the cleanliness of their home as ladies. Remember, you are trying to see your home *through her eyes*. Grab a vacuum cleaner and use it.

Dr. Kevin Leman wrote a fantastic book titled *Sex Begins in the Kitchen: Creating Intimacy to Make Your Marriage Sizzle.* Dr. Leman begins his book with a fictitious story about a family that runs out of the house following dinner. As the lady is driving back into the garage, and is hoping to just collapse in exhaustion, she remembers the dirty dishes that everyone just left behind. The next morning's activities will not allow her to let them wait. She is dreading the task, but decides to get it out of the way. When she walks in, she finds a clean kitchen and her husband hanging up the dish towels in the laundry room.[2] This is a perfect example of a man who saw the world through his wife's eyes and took action. Even if your division of responsibilities in the home is reasonably fair, and it is not your turn to do a task, jump on that task and enjoy her surprise. You might have an opportunity for sex to begin . . . and end right there in that kitchen. So, sweep that floor! She will not want it to be dirty.

Prayer: *LORD, help me to avoid the temptation to exhaust all of my energies working outside the house and neglect to reserve sufficient resources for my family responsibilities. Help me recognize ways to take initiative around my house in ways that will practically communicate my love and my commitment to my wife. Amen.*

Chapter 6

Money: Power House or Power Struggle

In our world, money is power. If you don't have enough money, you do not have enough power to legally bring food home from the grocery store, or complete most any task. In Chapter Five, we discovered that it is very important to reserve enough energy to assure you can participate in the household chores. It is equally important that you work with your spouse to ensure that your home is financially secure. *Financial security is romantic*, if the money is used in the right way.

Many people have said that money will not make you happy. That is true. I also assert that the lack of money can make you miserable. Certainly, one's attitude is the deciding factor, but constantly struggling with obtaining basic necessities is exhausting. When you add small children who can't provide for themselves into that equation, you have the potentiality of real struggle. Parents should not be at peace when their family members lack basic necessities.

In order to achieve financial security, you must work with your wife by partnering with her to achieve mutually agreed upon financial goals. You have invested your lives into each other. Therefore, it is imperative that you invest your resources together. If you don't have a written financial plan, then that must be your next priority. Make sure your tithe is in the budget. Remember: 90% plus faith is more secure than 100% plus nothing! Also, include an amount of "blow money" for yourself and your spouse. This is money you can each use at your own discretion without having to give account of it to your spouse. Utilize the resources provided by Dave Ramsey (daveramsey.com) or Joe Sangl (iwasbrokenowimnot.com). If you and your wife are not on the same page financially, then you will struggle with each other about how to use your power in our world. That disagreement can easily sabotage all other efforts toward marital romance.

Likewise, if you are in a very positive situation financially, how you spend your money will reveal your values. Marilyn Monroe famously sang "Diamonds are a girl's best friend" in the movie Gentlemen Prefer Blondes.[1] Nothing could be further from the truth. A diamond is a rock. It may be a pretty rock, but a rock none the less. If you have the resources to buy your wife a diamond every day, and you don't spend time with her and partner with her in the joys and struggles of life, then you will have an unhappy wife. . . for as long as she remains committed to you. That may not be very long.

So, where is the balance between working at home, and working to produce income? I assert that the balance is found in the mutually affirmed written budget that you made with your wife. If you and your wife have those written financial goals, then you can determine how much money you need to make as a couple in order to meet those financial goals. Beyond that, your time should be invested in ways that will create a legacy.

In a very broad sense, children will accept themselves in ways that they experience their mother's acceptance of them. Likewise, children will expect to be accepted by their peers in ways that mirror the level of acceptance they experienced from their dad. Additionally, the amount of *quality time* you spend with your wife will strongly influence her beliefs about how valuable she is to you. Billy Graham said, "The greatest legacy one can pass on to one's children and grandchildren is not money or other material things accumulated in one's life, but rather a legacy of character and faith."[2] Just like your wife and diamonds, children want your time, not the stuff you can buy because you gave the time they desired most to someone else. Giving time to your children, in appropriate balance with other responsibilities, will cause your wife to be happy that she invested her life in you. My friend, that is romance.

Prayer: *LORD, help me develop an understanding of the right work-life balance that you ordained for me. Help my wife and me to live within our means, and use the "power" we earn in ways that honor our family, and glorify you. Amen.*

Chapter 7

Loyalty

The family is the foundational building block of society. Families are like churches; they are never perfect because they are always filled with humans. However, family is the best solution for meeting the physical, emotional, financial, relational, and spiritual needs of adults while also providing a positive environment in which the next generation can grow.

If you have children, or have ever spent any time around a new-born baby, you know that they are 100% dependent on you or some other individual. They scream and you must figure out what they need and give it to them. Sometimes they are hungry. Sometimes they have a full diaper. Sometimes they need to be burped. Sometimes they have diaper rash. Sometimes they . . . Sometimes they . . . Sometimes they. .. .

As the child grows, he or she begins to be able to do more and more things for him-or herself. Therefore, the balance between his or her dependence on you and his or her independence begins to shift. The child wants more and more freedom to do things his or her own way. *It is the parent's job to give the child as much freedom that his or her maturity level and their recent behaviors have earned.* Teens are so eager to have all of the freedom in their lives, but they do not want the responsibility that level of freedom requires.

Once this older teen or young adult reaches some level of real independence, he or she begins to couple with others toward a goal of marriage. Often, he or she will couple with different individuals until they find the one they determine to be "Mr." or "Mrs." Right. Hopefully they are truly independent before coupling permanently because this begins the process of *interdependence*. Interdependence is the process by which individuals work together because they can accomplish more as a team than either of them can accomplish solo. They will do some things independently, but they begin a process through which they depend on each other for the basic necessities of life.

When you chose to marry your wife, this is the commitment you made. Your wife depends on you. This is why loyalty is so important and why divorce is so painful. Disloyalty rips apart the very canvas of life on which all of the family members have been painting. Unfortunately, sometimes divorce is necessary, but should only be chosen as an absolute last resort.

Your loyalty is one of those things that your spouse must experience in order for your efforts toward traditional romance to have a chance at making a positive impact. *Therefore, loyalty is romantic.* T.D. Jakes said, "Love does not really prove itself over romantic dinners or nice clothes. It proves itself in adversity."[1] Being there through adversity is a part of that environment you must create in order for your spouse to grow and become all that God created her to be.

Prayer: *LORD, Help me to remember that life always has adversity. Help me, in the name of Jesus, to refuse to use adversity in my marriage as an excuse to excuse my commitment of loyalty to my marriage and my family. Amen.*

Chapter 8

Is Her Body Mine?

As a Christian, I believe that the Bible is the guide by which Christians should pattern life. This is certainly true when it comes to your marriage and the romance in your marriage. However, the biblical hermeneutic, which is the process by which the Bible is interpreted, is very very important. In order to clearly understand how to apply many passages in the Bible to our lives, we must understand the context into which it was written. Then, we can determine the passage's application. Without that, you really can justify some things that are not God's way for marriage.

For example, in verses 3 and 4 of the 7th chapter of 1 Corinthians, Paul makes the following statement: "The husband should fulfill his wife's sexual needs, and the wife should fulfill her husband's needs. The wife gives authority over her body to her husband, and the husband gives authority over his body to his wife."[1] Without looking at the context into which this statement was written, a person could use this Scripture to justify marital rape! Let's look at the context.

Corinth was like modern-day Las Vegas. It was sin city for sure. Maritime travelers looked forward to docking in Corinth. In fact, in the Greek language, the word *korinthiazesthai* is translated "to live like a Corinthian" meaning one would live with consistent drunkenness and sexual immorality.[2] The society was very male chauvinistic, and men often only had sex with their wives for conception. For pleasurable sex, the men would go to one of the sexual prostitutes at Aphrodite's Temple. These prostitutes, who were more accurately described as sex slaves, were in side-by-side stalls that were not much bigger than a modern-day bathroom stall. Above the stall was a painting that depicted the sexual specialty of that particular individual.[3] How is that for romance? This sexual act had obviously physical significance for the man, but it also had a religious significance as well.

In that cultural backdrop, there was an argument in the Church regarding two schools of thought. Both of these ideas were based around the teaching of gnosticism, which influenced many religious belief systems of the ancient world. The term *gnosis* referred to religiously-based insight or knowledge, and the idea that matter, or one's physical body, was evil and separate from the spirit. In the Christian context, some people began to teach the idea that the knowledge of Jesus is all that was required for salvation. Therefore, they were free to continue in the highly-sexualized lifestyle as long as they had the knowledge of Jesus. William Barclay defined this teaching as follows: "If the body is evil, then it does not matter what a man does with it. The body is of no importance; all that matters is the spirit. Therefore, let a man glut and sate his appetites; these things are of no importance, and therefore a man can use his body in the most licentious and unbridled way and it makes no difference."[4] The second idea was that their bodies, and all of its desires, were wrong and must be avoided completely. This was true for married couples also.

In 1st Corinthians 7:1, Paul began a new section in his letter with "Now, regarding the questions you asked about." We do not have a copy of letter that the Corinthians wrote to Paul. We can assume that there were some married couples that wanted to have sex with each other, but were choosing to refrain from this due to the above-mentioned gnostic teaching. Paul clearly indicates, in the passage mentioned, that sex within the boundaries of marriage is acceptable, and sex outside of marriage is not. Paul also acknowledges that refraining from sex within marriage opens a door for sexual immorality outside of the marriage.

Therefore, the question becomes this: Do you have biblical authority to require your wife to have sex with you? I assert that you do not. In verse 6, Paul clearly indicates that his statement about this is "as a concession, not as a command." Paul did not command your wife to have sex with you. Paul, in the Corinthian context, allowed your wife the opportunity to "give authority over her body to her husband."

As a marriage and family therapist, I have never met a woman that enjoyed sex that was required by her husband based on this passage.

Remember this: Sex for ladies is much more about the relationship outside of the bedroom than it is about trying to make each other's eyeballs roll and face light up like a slot machine about to payout the jackpot. *Honoring your wife's choices about sexuality is romantic.* If your wife's primary love language is physical touch, please understand that physical touch is not just about sex. For many ladies, the love language is best expressed in non-sexual touch. If you want your wife to want to have sex with you, then you must focus on seeing the world through her eyes, and creating an environment in which she can grow and become all God created her to be. Find out how she wants to be touched, and when she wants to be touched in those ways. Sex is a physical celebration that can occur between two people who are experiencing a quality relationship. Touch wisely.

Prayer: *LORD, sometimes I feel like I am in Corinth because our culture advertises almost every product with a mostly naked attractive woman. The availability of sexualized material is so rampant. Yet, I trust that your design for my sexual needs is best for me. Help me to love my wife sexually in a way that causes her to feel cherished, honored, sexy, adored, and absolutely beautiful. Amen.*

Chapter 9

Manage Your Emotions

A few years ago, I worked with a young man who gave me permission to share this story with you. He struggled with an anxiety disorder, and he came into my office with a tense look on his face. I asked him about his anxiety. He said, "Well, if you give me a piece of coal, I can shove it up my a** and make you a diamond." You must admit that describes someone that is really uptight. I hope I never forget that story. In some ways, I feel like I owe that young man some money back for that session because that statement tickled my funny bone to the point that I don't think I really gave him quality care that day.

How you manage your emotions significantly contributes to the environment of your home. I am confident you have walked into a room and felt the tension that could be "cut with a knife" as the old saying highlights. No one needs to say a word, but you can feel it. If you do not manage your stress from your work outside of the home, you dump that into the environment of your home. If you do not manage your emotional reactions to events that occur in your home, then you create new problems in your home based solely on how you choose to express.

Imagine a fictitious family. The husband and father has an explosive temper, and something happened that royally ticked him off. Impulsively, he punches a wall. He justifies this to himself by saying that it is better to punch a wall than punch his child or his wife. Domestic violence is never the right answer. Yet, even the smallest child can figure out that Dad was angry enough to punch, and he or she may be next. Remember, "punches" can happen physically, verbally, and a variety of other ways.

The easiest way to evaluate the management of your emotions is to look at the results of your expressions. If you punch a wall, you now have a hole in the wall to repair, and potentially a broken hand. That is two new problems that did not exist prior to you expressing your feelings. If your expressions create new problems for yourself or your loved ones, then they need to be changed.

My Dad used to play golf with a fellow pastor who would determine which of his parishioners had made him angry that week. Then, he would write the name of that person on his golf ball, and smack it all over the course. Notice, no one was even aware, but the pastor was able to aggressively express his anger. Personally, when I get very angry, I go to a driving range and hit golf balls. I pretend that little white ball is my problem and I send it as far away as possible. I enjoy playing golf. You need to find something that you can enjoy that also has a way to express your anger or other emotions physically and aggressively.

Above, I mentioned times when you might have walked into a room and you could feel the tension in the room. You must also remember that even small children can feel it. I once worked with a family that had a very small child that was still crawling. The couple brought the young man into the session with them because they could not afford a baby sitter. During the session, the child could sense the tension as the mother was expressing her anger at her spouse in a very vocally volatile manner. The child was sitting in his dad's lap, and started to squirm. The child was not old enough to understand the words, but he could feel the struggle between the two people that he loved the most. He squirmed out of his dad's lap and crawled over to his mother. She picked him up, and the child immediately slapped his mother right across the face. That was the child's way of demanding that the mother treat the dad with respect.

There is a difference in managing your emotions and stuffing your emotions. Often men hold their emotions until they explode. Allow me to illustrate this point by asking you a question: What would happen if you decided to stop going to the bathroom? When you go to the bathroom, your body is releasing infection. If you hold that inside, it will eventually get into your blood stream, travel to each organ in your body, and you can and probably will die. Much more likely is the probability that you will make a big mess. Emotions are the same. If you hold them inside, they will either make you sick, usually in the form of depression or anxiety, or you will have an emotional outburst in ways that create chaos for yourself and everyone around you.

You can't get away from the fact that the environment you create is the environment in which your children do not have legal option to leave, unless you are legally abusive. Your wife has the option to leave, and if you do not manage your emotions appropriately, her maternal instinct will motivate her to leave so that she can protect your children and herself from you. *Managing your emotions is romantic* in the sense that your family will not enjoy a quality environment if your emotional outbursts or obvious unspoken tension is something you consistently dump in their lap.

Prayer: *LORD, help me to identify the emotions that I feel, and express them in ways that are respectful to all, and do not create new problems for myself or others. Amen.*

Chapter 10

Supporting Her Hopes and Dreams

Have you ever been to a church or other organization that has individuals who want things to "go back to the way they used to be"? Often times people get stuck always thinking about the past. Do you recognize that if you spend a significant amount of time thinking about the way it used to be, regardless of the context, you are focusing your energy on doing nothing today, and not even dreaming about how things will be better tomorrow?

Think for a moment, if you will about Bill Gaither. He and his wife Gloria have written numerous songs that are standards in Southern Gospel Music. In 1991, at the age of 55, Gaither was producing an album that was a tribute to many of the pioneers of Southern Gospel Music. At that time, Gaither had already won 2 Grammy Awards, and 19 dove awards. His biography, written by himself and Ken Abraham, states that he was thinking of retiring. However, for this above-mentioned album, he invited some of those pioneers of Southern Gospel Music to take a picture for the album art. They took the picture around a piano, and then they started to sing.[1] Gaither had a video crew there to record the event for his own archives. He later decided to allow a Christian TV station to air it. There were so many calls to purchase that video, Gaither decided to make another one.[2] Currently, Gaither and those "pioneers" as well as many new faces in Gospel and Contemporary Christian Music, have enjoyed a complete revival of their music careers. Do you think any of that would have occurred without the support of his wife Gloria? Since 1991, Gaither has won four additional Grammy Awards, 21 additional Dove Awards, and along with his supportive wife the title Christian Songwriter of the Century by The American Society of Composers and Publishers.[3]

What about your wife? Does she have your support to reinvent herself? Can she chase her dreams and know that you will be right by her side?

Imagine your wife receiving a vision of ministry from God. What if her dreams or calling from God require you to take on an unequal share of the household responsibilities, or adjust your life in some other way? Remember, she has invested her life into you, and she deserves to know that you will also invest your life into her, regardless of where that road takes you. *Supporting her hopes and dreams is romantic.*

Prayer: LORD, *help me to pay attention to the dreams, aspirations, and hope that you have placed inside my bride. Help me to know how to follow your leadership in ways that her dreams and goals will be reached. Amen.*

Chapter 11

Quality Time

The amount of energy that a person has for an activity is directly correlated to the amount of desire the person has for that activity. Zig Ziglar illustrated this point with the following fictitious story: A man is at home and his wife suggests that today is a good day for him to clean out the garage like he has been promising to do. His reaction to that suggestion is colored by his lack of desire to do it. Therefore, he explains to his wife that he is just "too tired." The man begins to walk around the house looking exhausted and pitiful. A short time later, the phone rings, and the caller is one of the man's friends who is asking him to go play 18 holes at their local golf course. Suddenly this man has all the energy he needs to walk almost 6 miles on the course, and swing a club somewhere between 70 and 110 times![1]

So, what changed? The only difference in to two scenarios is that the man wanted to play golf, and wanted to spend time with his friends. How would you feel if your wife had energy to do things with others and did not have energy to do things with you, or accomplish tasks which eliminate stress and struggle for both of you?

Dr. Gary Chapman states that quality time is one of the five primary love languages.[2] How you chose to spend your time, and with whom you chose to spend your time will communicate to your wife the level of priority she is in your life. In chapter 2, I made the following statement: In order for her to feel that she is still in your heart, the expression must be initiated by you, and come from your heart. Quality time is a perfect example of that statement. *Quality Time is romantic.* If you don't initiate quality time with your wife, why would you think that she would feel like you value her as a person? Every relationship, including a marital relationship, needs time apart so that you each have an opportunity to spread your wings and have an opportunity to miss each other. Yet, if you do not prioritize quality time as a couple, then all of your other activities that are designed to meet your wife's needs, especially romantic needs, will be as ineffective as a fire truck that has gasoline in its water tank. No matter how hard you work spraying the fire with the fire hose, the lack of your response to her actual need (quality time) will eventually cause the situation to blow up in your face.

Prayer: *LORD, help me to understand my wife's need for my time. Renew my desire to spend time with her in ways that create the excitement of the love we shared early in our relationship, while maintaining the security that our history together has earned. Give me your insight into the person that she is, and help me to love her with the same passion with which you love her. Amen.*

Chapter 12

The Little Things

Dale Carnegie was already a published author in 1934 when Leon Shimkin came to one of the classes that he taught. Carnegie was teaching a 14-week class titled "Public Speaking and Influencing Men in Business." Shimkin, who represented Simon & Schuster Publishing Company, encouraged Carnegie to write a book titled *The Art of Getting Along with People.* Having been turned down by Simon & Schuster twice before, Carnegie at first refused. Shimkin was persistent, and two years later Carnegie submitted the manuscript now titled *How to Win Friends and Influence People.* The book is based on Carnegie's ideas about being successful in the business world. Four months following the publication date, the book had sold 333,000 copies, and Carnegie's first royalty check was for $90,000, which is equal to over 1.5 million dollars today. Currently, Simon & Schuster have sold over 30 million copies of this book.[1] This book is considered by many to be the first self-help book, and if you have not read this book, make it your next read, (after you finish reading the book in your hands, of course.)

Carnegie states the following: "You can make more friends in two months by becoming interested in other people than you can in two years by trying to get other people interested in you."[2] What about your wife? How often do you show genuine interest in her? I am not talking about when you want something from her, need something from her, or need her to take care of something for you. Remember, she has invested her life into you.

In 1981, Carnegie's company revised and updated Carnegie's classic book that was published so many years prior. In that edition, two sections were removed. One of those sections was titled "Seven Rules for Making Your Home Life Happier." In the original editions, Carnegie indicated that "little attentions" are a must for every marriage. He states, "The meaning of little attentions is this: it shows the person you love that you are thinking of her, that you want to please her, and that her happiness and welfare are very dear and very near to your heart."[3]

Seriously, in today's world, how long does it take to communicate with your wife when you are physically in different locations. If your wife's love language is words of affirmation, there is really no excuse for not taking time to communicate those affirmations. You can send a text in a matter of seconds. You can type a simple phrase like "I love you", "I miss you", or "I am ready for date night" into the search engine of your phone. Then select images and you will have hundreds of little images you can save to your phone and quickly send it to your wife.

Why do Christians pray before meals? Some say that physical hunger can be used as a reminder to thank God for God's provision. Well, this book is written with the idea that you can read a chapter during the time you are sitting on your throne. What if you decided to use your own need to go to the bathroom as a reminder to send a text message to your wife that indicates she is on your mind. Please, don't tell her that you are using your bowel movements as a reminder to think about her! Yet, going to the bathroom is something you probably will not forget to do. Therefore, make it a reminder to communicate a simple "You are on my mind" kind of message. It will take seconds, and pay dividends that last a lifetime. *Little attentions are romantic.*

Prayer: LORD, Help me to value my wife's need to hear from me on a regular basis. Teach me to say the things that help her to be assured of my love. Teach me to love her in a way that makes her excited that she invested her life into me. Amen.

Chapter 13

Date Night

Usually, when a couple first comes into my office, they both have a story to tell. I will give them some time to share. Once they have expressed their perspectives on the problem, I will often ask them about the last time that they went on a date . . . just the two of them. Often, the couple will look at each other with an incredulous look on each of their faces, and one of them will break the awkward silence by saying something like, "We went out to dinner a few weeks ago." "What did you discuss?" would be my next question. Another awkward silence is broken by one of them suggesting that they discussed something about their children.

Couples often lose their feelings of connectedness with each other when they stop prioritizing "alone time" with each other. Certainly, children are important and need your attention. However, if you neglect your marriage in favor of the children, you will create a scenario in which the children feel they are responsible for the distance between Mom and Dad. In fact, children can't understand adult issues, and when Mom and Dad separate and divorce, because they neglected their marriage, children often blame themselves and falsely identify something they did to cause the divorce. Therefore, you are doing the best thing you can for your children when you prioritize time as a couple which purposefully excludes them. They also need time away from you to develop their independence and individuation. Therefore, if date time must be prioritized, what is the next step?

You need to change your mind, to expand your mind, about what it means to have a date. A date can last five minutes or five days. A date can cost hundreds to thousands of dollars, or it can be completely free. A date can be at home, or in an exotic location. There are not any limits to dating. The purpose of a date is to have scheduled time in which you and your spouse purposefully connect and re-connect with each other.

This is where your creativity comes in. Part of romance is investment. It is investment of time. It is investment of thought. It is investment of resources. It is investment of your heart. Use your creativity to create a situation in which these investments have an opportunity to grow. Here is an exercise:

Walk up to your wife and ask her to go on a date with you. Let her know the time that the date will begin, assuming that time works in her schedule. Let her know the type of attire or clothing she will need to be wearing, and the approximate time you will bring her home. Tell her that you will arrange everything else, and it will be a surprise. Then, make yourself a list of things you need to do. For example, arrange for childcare, make reservations for whatever activity in which you will be engaging, plan for some unscheduled time so that the two of you can be spontaneous (if desired), and ensure that you plan an activity that works with both of your personalities as well as the state of your relationship. If your relationship is struggling, you are not going to get it back on track by planning one night of candlelight dinner in an expensive restaurant. Remember, this is where you must see the world "Through Her Eyes."

So, you have the time reserved in her schedule, the child care is arranged, and you now need to decide on what to do next. You must use your creativity, but you can use other sources for ideas. Put something like "romantic ideas" in your search engine and see what you like or what would match your wife's personality. Look at the local businesses in a 50-mile area, and see how they might be a part of your investment into your marriage. Assuming your wife still wants to have the connection with you, then you only have to open the door for her.

Here are a few ideas:

- Go for a walk and have a few discussion topics selected
- If she is athletic, do a fun sporting activity
- Take her to be pampered
- Take her on a dinner cruise
- Proactively look at her unmet needs and meet them

- Be willing to be vulnerable enough to share your real struggles and joys of life with her, and MORE IMPORTANTLY, LISTEN to her joys and struggles of life.

Remember: Romance is not something you can fake. If you are trying to do all the "right things" so you can get what you want in the end, your wife will most likely see through your game. You must be real! I do not mean that you have to get mushy and emotional. You do have to affirm who you are, how important she is to you, and how you look forward to sharing the future with her. In her environment, she needs your time, your attention, your love, and your affection. She is not someone that you can simply replace. She is the one that God ordained for you. She is your fruitful vine.

Once your date night is over, ask your wife if she would be willing to plan the next date. The goal is for you to have a date night once a week, and you alternate planning and being surprised. This allows both of you to plan and both of you to be surprised every other week. Don't let anything get in the way of date night. If there is a conflict in the schedule, use your creativity to plan around it. Your wife needs to understand through your actions, that she is a priority to you. Act accordingly. *Dating is romantic.*

Prayer: *LORD, Help me to prioritize time with my wife in a way that allows us to continue to enjoy each other. I appreciate the wonderful gift you gave to me when you ordained our relationship. Teach me to continue to love her with your unconditional love, with erotic love, with friendship love, and with family love. Amen.*

Chapter 14

Unexpected Surprises

Surprises are a great way to reveal that you are thinking about your wife. A surprise does not have to cost money. It is simply something that she is not expecting. If you never give a surprise, then life is going to get quite boring. No one enjoys the feeling of being "in a rut." There is a famous quote that has been attributed to George Carlin, Maya Angelou, Vicki Corona, Hilary Cooper, and maybe others. The true originator of the quote is unknown or at least disputed. However, that does not take away from the power of the quote: "Life is not measured by the number of breaths you take, but by the moments that take [y]our breath away."[1]

Surprises are romantic! I strongly suggest that you have a discussion with your wife about surprises and honesty. In order to pull off a good surprise, such as a surprise birthday party or other fun activity, you may not need or be able to be 100% open and honest. Yet, you do not want to violate her trust. So, ensure that you and your wife are on the same page about this, providing that you both agree that 100% honesty must be restored following the surprise.

I imagine you are getting tired of me prompting you to be creative. Remember: Romance is using your own creativity to express the love that is in your heart in ways that will make her feel loved, honored, and cherished. When you say to yourself, and to your wife, that you are not creative enough to do this, she will hear you say that she is not important enough to you for you to put forth some effort and try. I am sure that is not a message you want to communicate. Engage your brain, and make it happen. It is a skill. The more you do it, the more your skill will increase. The only way to completely fail is to not do it at all.

What is something simple, that your wife would not expect you to do, something that will help your wife see that you were thinking about her or seeing the world through her eyes? To do this, think about the normal routine of your family. Think about your wife's recent experiences, such as her stress level at work, recent difficulties with your kids, or some other struggle that she has been enduring. Then, think of something different that she will enjoy.

Here are a few suggestions:

- Send her a text: "Baby, I know you have been working hard, and I so appreciate all you do. Tonight, I would like for you to take the night off. The kids and I will do all the cooking and cleaning. We want you to just relax."
- Have a bouquet of flowers delivered to her work. This is especially good if she works with a group of ladies. Not only will she enjoy the time and attention that you put into getting the flowers, she will also enjoy the other ladies doting over her because her man was romantic.
- Take the day off from work and do not tell her. When she arrives home, you have completed all the housework, and cooked dinner.
- Put aside some of your "blow money" each month and purchase an unexpected Christmas gift.
- Show up at her work with bags packed and a weekend getaway already planned.

Surprises do not have to be difficult. They require a few minutes of thought. A few minutes of planning, and a little creativity. Yet, they will keep your wife guessing about what you will do next. That time you invest, and the interest she invests will keep your marriage moving in the right direction.

Prayer: LORD, *help me to have confidence in my own ability to be creative. I want to stay alert to opportunities for surprises, and take advantage of them in ways that will communicate my love for my wife. I affirm you as the source of love. Help me to love with total abandon, just as you did for me. Amen.*

Chapter 15

Meet Needs Without Prompting

Let's get real for a moment: Some men mistake their wife for their mother, and they forget that they are a grown man. Throughout this book, we have mostly been talking about her needs. In this chapter, we are going to talk about your own needs. However, we are not talking about how you can get her to meet your needs. It is time to have some direct conversation about how you need to meet your own needs. You are not a child. You can be interdependent (Chapter 7) without being dependent for your own basic needs, and you should not need her to prompt you to do it. You will meet one of her needs by taking care of yourself.

This may not apply to everyone that is reading this book; but based on my experiences doing therapy, I bet it applies to many of you. Why is it that some men have an expectation that their wives will do things for them that they are completely capable of doing themselves? As a husband, do you expect these chores to be done regardless of what is going on in your wife's life?

I once knew a couple who had lived the "traditional family" life for more than a decade. The lady was a stay-at-home mom, and the dad worked outside of the home. Once the children reached the teen years, the couple decided that the lady would go back to school and earn a degree that would eventually bring a second income into the home. Once she was in school, her time to complete household chores decreased significantly. The man started complaining because he did not have any underwear folded and in his underwear drawer. So, she did exactly what he demanded. She folded his underwear and placed them in his drawer. She just did not bother to wash them first. . . He got the message.

Over the next week, take time to notice how often you leave your clothes on the floor with an expectation of your wife picking them up. Take time to notice how often you leave dirty dishes. Take time to notice how often you leave a mess in the bathroom. *Meeting your own needs is romantic* to your wife because you are taking part in maintaining her environment in a way that works for her as well as yourself. Regardless of whether or not you and your wife have children, she does not need practice in parenting by taking care of the stuff you need. Clean up after yourself!

Prayer: *LORD, I recognize that I may be able to live in a home that my wife would call a disaster area. Yet, I am learning that it's not all about me. Teach me to have an open mind and see the trail of uncleanliness that I leave. Help me to discipline myself to pick up after myself. Amen.*

Chapter 16

Decision Making

Imagine every day hearing "HONEY, WHAT'S FOR DINNER?" Often times we men want to be the "man of the house" when it comes to making the big decisions. Yet, most often, it is the "little" or day-to-day decisions that make a home function. The stereotypical days where the man went to work and the woman remained at home are long gone. Yet, many men still want their wives to function as if she has been at home all day, even though she went to work like he did. Why should she always have to decide what is for dinner? Why should she need not only to decide what is for dinner, but also to prepare it? The dinner-table decisions are only an example of many day-to-day decisions that must be made for your family to function.

When you are at work, are you in any position of leadership? If so, you hopefully understand that leadership requires a variety of planning. You need a long-term plan of what your work will accomplish. You need a short-term plan of what you need to make progress on that long-term goal(s). You need a plan of action for today so that your actions match your goals. Apply that same type of logic to your home life.

For example, I imagine your long-term goal is to provide your family members food that is nutritious and also tasty. Is it your wife's job to make weekly menus that accomplish that goal (short-term goal)? Is it always your wife's job to actually prepare the food that will accomplish this goal (daily plan of action.)? In order for this goal to be achieved, you must plan, accomplish short-term goals, as well as daily plans of action.

Now expand your mind by thinking about other day-to-day things in your house that require planning actions. If you join your wife in those long-term goals, short-term planning, and day-to-day actions, she will feel your partnership in everyday life. That will make her glad that she invested in you. *Joint decision making and implementation is romantic.*

Prayer: LORD, *Help me to continue to open my own mind to ways that I can serve my wife in the way you would have me to serve her. Amen.*

Chapter 17

Show Her Your Strength

Sometimes life has difficulties. In difficult times, people will occasionally misquote Scripture and say something like "God will not put more on you than you can handle." The Bible does not really say that. The verse being referred to in this context is 1 Corinthians 10:13. "The temptations in your life are no different than what other's experience. And God is faithful. He will not allow the temptation to be more than you can stand. When you are tempted, he will show you a way out so that you can endure."[1]. This verse does not say that you will not have difficult problems that are more than you can handle on your own. It indicates that you will not be tempted. Sometimes we are impacted by the choices of others, or the existence of something undesired which impacts us — but we did not do anything to cause the situation in which we find ourselves.

Chris Jenkins, and his incredible wife Dianne, continue to endure such a situation. On October 25th, 1996, Chris and Dianne welcomed their son, Tate, into this world. Seventeen years later, while enduring a battle with bipolar disorder, Tate often attempted to self-medicate with harmful recreational drugs. The chaos of that struggle brought Tate to a very difficult place, and Tate took his own life. Chris and Dianne had done everything in their power to save their beloved son from his struggles. Yet, Tate made a choice, and the impact of that choice will forever continue.

Chris knew that a very high percentage of parents who lose a child in death end up also losing their marriage because the stress of the loss and the reminders of grief that the spouses unintentionally create becomes more than some can bear. He voiced his intention to me that he would not allow that to happen in his marriage. Yet, even though he is a pastor, he and Dianne struggled with the same questions and cries out to God as others experience in a situation like this.

Chris needed something he could do that would help distract him from the constant unbearable grief. Chris is very good with his hands. He started looking for people with homes that needed some form of repair and he offered to help. He quickly realized that many homes in his area had very insufficient insulation. As a result, the tenants of those homes had very high electric bills. Yet, the landlords would not do anything about it.

God spoke to Chris with a vision of a new ministry called Hope Restorations. This ministry began with people who have a short time of sobriety, and have burned most of their bridges in past relationships. Chris took the desire he had to continue to help Tate and applied that to those who continue to struggle as Tate did. Chris then paired those individuals with the tenants who lived in homes with poor insulation.

Initially, Chris began to teach the individuals, who recently established sobriety, how to install insulation. This helped the tenants lower their electric bills, and provided a job reference for those doing the installation work. The ministry has grown to the point that they are now doing a wide variety of projects that benefit the community. Currently, Hope Restorations has been granted a 501c3 non-profit status. It's board of directors has elected Chris as the Executive Pastor for this ministry. It has been given financial resources from the Duke Endowment, and continues to provide a fantastic ministry to the community. The ministry's purpose statement is as follows: "The purpose of the corporation is to provide employment, training, recovery support and other assistance to adults recovering from addictions while improving or providing safe, comfortable, and more energy efficient housing to struggling families in our area." Effective June 1, 2017, Chris left his parish based ministry, and moved into this role on a full-time basis. The United Methodist Church recognizes Hope Restorations as an extension ministry of the UMC. It is wonderful to hear Chris tell of experiences like taking a piece of plywood and laying it across two saw horses for a make shift communion table on a construction site. Hope Restorations is teaching the grace of Jesus to adults in recovery. Hope Restorations is giving a loving hand to people who struggle for necessities. Hope

Restorations is restoring hope. Chris leaned on God and found strength that God provided. He has a way to channel his grief positively, and this continues to be a piece of the puzzle that protects his marriage.[2]

Franklin D. Roosevelt said, "Courage is not the absence of fear, but rather the assessment that something else is more important than fear."[3] Chris Jenkins realized that his marriage was more important than his fear of the grief. Chris is one of the strongest men I know. I offer his example to you as evidence that sometimes God does allow more than you can handle on your own. If we can handle everything life can throw at us without needing any help from God or anyone else, then we don't need God. You can't go through the struggles of life on your own. Lean on God, and allow His strength to strengthen you. Then, you can be someone on which your wife can also lean. *Strength, in all types of crises, is romantic!* Show her your strength in that you will stay with her and she can count on you. Show her your strength in that you will do all you can do to provide for your family. Show her your strength by purposefully leading your family in a way that honors God, honors your wife, honors your children, and is a positive example in the community.

Prayer: For this chapter's prayer, I offer you the full version of a prayer written by theologian Reinhold Niebuhr. The first verse of this prayer became well known through the meetings of Alcoholics Anonymous. It is known as the Serenity Prayer:

God, give us grace to accept with serenity
the things that cannot be changed,
Courage to change the things
which should be changed,
and the Wisdom to distinguish
the one from the other.

Living one day at a time,
Enjoying one moment at a time,

Accepting hardship as a pathway to peace,
Taking, as Jesus did,
This sinful world as it is,
Not as I would have it,
Trusting that You will make all things right,
If I surrender to Your will,
So that I may be reasonably happy in this life,
And supremely happy with You forever in the next. [4]

Amen.

Chapter 18

Emotionally Vulnerable Is Not Weakness

In Chapter 17, we discussed strength and the fact that it is not directly tied to one's emotion. Some things are more important than just your emotions. Yet, that does not mean that your emotions do not have a place. Many men have been taught that "boys don't cry." The truth, though, is it is very unhealthy to hold your emotions inside. (See chapter 9).

From the beginning, I promised you that I would not try to make you think that you have lost or should turn in your "man card." Yet, in order to be romantic, you must connect with your own heart in a way that allows you to "be real." If you set an example in your home that indicates that emotions are not acceptable, allowed, or desired, you will teach your children and your wife that you provide, but you are not really available.

Think for a moment about a theater mask. This is the type that is commonly referred to as Greek Tragedy masks because they used them to depict different characters or different emotions. Take a moment and think about the "mask" that you wear each day. What do you want the expressions on your mask to communicate? Do you often have a happy face, a peaceful face, or a content face? More often than not, when we are experiencing difficult emotions, we have facial expressions that we do not realize we are portraying.

What about "behind your mask"? Imagine for a moment that you are actually wearing a mask, and this mask is painting exactly as you desire to portray yourself. Now, reach up and place your hand on your imaginary mask. Pull it away, and look inside the mask. Look at the space that was just touching your face. Imagine that this side of the mask is painted to be an exact representation of how you feel. Do you feel anxious, angry, tired, sad, jealous, bored, or confused? From a mental health perspective, the goal is to have the outside and the inside of the mask to match.

From a marital perspective, these emotions which follow the joys and struggles of life are one of the things that your wife wants from you. In order to experience life with you, she must be able to see the real you. It is not weakness to be vulnerable. *Being emotionally vulnerable and available is romantic.* Your wife will most likely see it as a strength.

Prayer: *LORD, I recognize that you are the perfect example of strength and simultaneous vulnerability. When you went to pray in the Garden of Gethsemane, you were so "scared and emotional" that your sweat became blood. Yet, you knew that some things are more important than your feelings, your pain, and your life. With my family, help me to follow your example in a way that will point them to you. Amen.*

Chapter 19

Honesty

Do you remember Bernie Madoff? For most people the mention of his name brings feelings of distrust, anger, and being deceived. Mr. Madofff was a well-respected financier, and he even was a part of a group of business professionals that started the NASDAQ. However, rather than being honest about the returns he was gaining on his client's investments, he used a ponzi scheme. Mr. Madoff promised his client's a very high return on their investment and then used the money of other investors to make up the difference between the actual returns and the promised returns. This type of scheme can go on for as long as the deceptive schemer has more new investments than requested returns.[1] In Mr. Madoff's case, he accepted 20 billion dollars in investments, and provided statements to his clients that indicated they collectively had received a total of 65 billion in returns. Not only did Mr. Madoff not gain the promised 45 billion in returns as indicated by his statements to his clients, he also lost the original investments through his lavish lifestyle and his process of using one investor's money to pay the dividends to another investor. As of the date of this writing, only 11.576 billion of the original 20 billion dollars that were invested has been recovered.[2]

It is my sincere hope that you were not personally involved in the above-mentioned investment scheme. However, I want you to take a moment and think about all of the money you have in savings, investments, and other types of interest-bearing accounts. What if all, or at least the vast majority, of your money was suddenly gone, and there was really not anything you could do to get it back. Now think about your wife.

On the day that your wife said "I do" to you, she invested not only her financial resources, but more importantly her dreams, hopes, and desires. She invested in you as the father or step-father of her children. She invested in you as the one with whom she wants to share the day-to-day joys and struggles of life. If you are deceptive to her, or living a double life, then you are being as two-faced as Bernie Madoff. Are you honest with her about all the money or debt you have? Are you honest with her about where you go, and with whom you spend time? Are you honest with her about all of your online activity? Is there any part of your life that would be a hurtful surprise to her if she found out?

Now, imagine for a moment that you have a new investment account. Every deposit increases the value. Likewise, every withdrawal decreases it's worth. Being trustworthy and the person you claimed to be are deposits. Your wife's belief in you is the interest on those deposits. However, your wife discovering that you are deceptive is a major withdrawal that will take your account to a very negative balance. Just like a bank account, deposits can eventually eliminate the negative balance. Trust in relationships can be earned again, as long as the withdrawal does not end the relationship. Yet, your balance will never be what it could have been if that big withdrawal was never made. *Honesty is romantic* in the sense that it is a requirement for all other parts of the relationship to function in a healthy way. You must be honest in the good stuff and the struggles. Proverbs 12:22 states, "The LORD detests lying lips, but he delights in those who tell the truth."[3]

Prayer: *LORD, help me to be totally honest with my wife. Sometimes it is hard because it requires that I am so vulnerable. Yet, she can't love all of me unless I show her all of me. Help me refrain from any activity about which I would want to deceive her. Help me to remember the investment she has made in me, and ensure that I hold the investment of her heart in a way that ensures her safety, and provides an honest return on her investment. Amen.*

Chapter 20

Develop a Spiritual Discipline

When you think about your relationship with God, is it reactive where you are waiting on God to do something to grab your attention? Is it indecisive, like a squirrel that stands in the middle of a highway looking to the left and right multiple times, but which ultimately stands still for far too long? Is your relationship proactive in the sense that you are taking responsibility to find new ways to learn more and more about the character of God and how to incorporate God into every aspect of your life?

The Apostle Paul established the first Christian Church in Europe in approximately 49 A.D. This was in a military retirement town called Philippi. About 10 years later, Paul is in prison and writes to the people in this congregation. Paul was facing the possibility that he would be executed. Being a Christian was a crime which was punishable by death, and a person could save their own life by recanting his faith in Jesus. Yet, Paul expresses that he is hopeful that he will never be "ashamed" of his faith.[1] Paul must have known that a very common type of execution was *Damnatio ad bestias* or damnation by beast. Paul was expressing hope that he could withstand the assault of a wild animal, such as a lion, and always remain true to his faith. Tradition tells us that Paul was executed, but it was done via beheading. So, a wild animal did not cause Paul's death, but he did not know that when he was writing this to the Philippians.[2]

Later in this same letter, Paul expresses his pedigree as a Jewish man. His credentials were very impressive. However, Paul describes all of those accomplishments as "garbage."[3] Have you taken the time to have a long look into a dumpster lately? Did you notice the aroma? Knowing that Paul considered his accomplishments to be garbage and his top priority was to hold on to the very thing that could send him to a very painful and long-suffering execution, it is impossible to say that Paul's faith was anything other than very proactive.

What about you? Fortunately, in the United States, we do not usually live under the threat of the type of persecution that was common in Paul's time. That type of persecution is active in our world, and it is more and more common here. Even though we generally are free to seek God in a proactive way, we take the freedom for granted, and then sit back and reactively wait on God. Are you at the point that you are ready to forget the past and look to a future that only seeks the high calling of Christ Jesus (Phil. 3:14)? If so, what are you proactively doing to prepare for that? Maybe you have been doing the same spiritual routine for years. This routine might include church attendance, Bible study, church activities, daily prayer, and/or other activities designed for spiritual growth. What if you proactively "pressed toward the mark" by developing a new spiritual discipline?

In 1978, Richard Foster worked between 12 and 15 hours per day for a 33-day period writing a book that was named by *Christianity Today* as one of the top ten books written in the 20th Century. This book is titled *Celebration of Discipline: The Path to Spiritual Growth*. Foster identifies the "inward disciplines" of the Christian life as prayer, fasting, meditation, and study. The "outward disciplines" are simplicity, solitude, submission, and service. The "corporate disciplines" are confession, worship, guidance, and celebration. If you are not aware of anything you can proactively do to increase the presence of God in your life, secure a copy of Foster's book, and read it. Once you have completed the entire book, go back and select one of the disciplines and implement it. Then repeat that process for the other disciplines. These proactive steps, along with ongoing Bible study, will help you care for your own soul and increase your joy of being a follower of Jesus Christ.

As a husband, father, and spiritual leader of your family, you cannot lead anyone to a spiritual place you have not been. From a Christian worldview, *developing a new spiritual discipline is romantic.*

Prayer: *LORD, help me to value my relationship with you to the point that I am proactive about it. Help me to see you working in my life, the lives of my family members, and the lives of people around me. Help me to notice ways that I can join what you are doing and help others in ways that also glorify you. Help me to be the leader I need to be in my family.*

Chapter 21

Thoughtful Gifts

What if you asked your wife to take Gary Chapman's love language profile, and it revealed that her love language is receiving gifts. Do you feel like a big whole just developed in your pocket, and your bank account can't support her love language? If that is your thought, then you need to eliminate that type of thinking. A gift does not have to be something that you buy!

On the 5lovelanguages.com website, the "gifts received" love language is defined: "Don't mistake this love language for materialism; the receiver of gifts thrives on the love, thoughtfulness, and effort behind the gift. If you speak this language, the perfect gift or gesture shows that you are known, you are cared for, and you are prized above whatever was sacrificed to bring the gift to you. A missed birthday, anniversary, or a hasty, thoughtless gift would be disastrous – so would the absence of everyday gestures. Gifts are visual representations of love and are treasured greatly."[1]

This is where your creativity must be utilized. Remember it is not the gift that creates the feeling of being loved. It is your effort. It is your investment. It is the obvious love in your heart that is expressed through the investment and effort required to create the gift that makes the difference. Your gift does not necessarily need to be materialistic, but it does often need to be material. It needs to be something that your wife can hold in her hand(s). For example, you could write your wife a love letter. For the cost of a stamp, and a few minutes of thought and effort, you could make her day.

Regardless of whether your wife's love language is receiving gifts or not, how much time, thought, and effort do you put into the gifts you do give her? Think about Christmas gifts, birthday gifts, or anniversary gifts. When do you start thinking about those gifts? If you wait until just before the gift needs to be given, you will inevitably give a gift that is hastily purchased.

Generally, many ladies drop hints about gifts they desire, and they will do this days, weeks, or months prior to the date the gift is given. It is a subtle way for them to check if you are really paying attention. So, step one in preparing to give a fantastic gift is to pay attention to all the things that she has to say. Getting the material item is not anywhere near as valuable to her as the fact that you listen and incorporate her wants and desires into your life. Your response is evidence of that.

Step two is put some of yourself into the gift. If you buy a gift that another person has created, you traded some of the time and effort you invested at your job for the item. Add something from your heart to the gift. You could add a card with a nice loving sentiment, or you can think of a clever way to present the gift; then again, you can even involve other loved ones in the gift giving.

Step three is to provide some element of surprise. Imagine a Christmas day and you already know every gift you will receive. There is no element of surprise, and you open box after box only to have your expectations met without any additional excitement. That is not the type experience your wife desires. She wants the "Wow!" factor. "Wow!" does not have to come in the form of an expensive gift, especially if she knows that you bought something you could not afford or something that put you even further in debt. That only makes her wonder how the debt will be paid. "Wow!" comes with ideas that are inexpensive to create, but priceless to those who receive them. *Thoughtful gifts are romantic.*

Prayer: *LORD, help me to learn to pay more attention to the daily expressions that my wife makes, and then learn to implement them into my life. Help me give gifts that reflect more of my heart than my wallet. Let your love for her be expressed through the gifts that I give. Amen.*

Chapter 22

Love Your Wife by Leading Your Children

Imagine yourself at work and you notice one of your co-workers, who is also a friend, just walking out of the building. Your supervisor comes to you and you can see the frustration on his or her face. He tells you that your co-worker just quit without notice, and you are now responsible for doing your job and his or her job. There is not a plan to hire someone to replace your co-worker, and in order to keep your job, you must do both jobs without a pay increase.

When couples separate and divorce, the above-mentioned story is often the experience of the parent that maintains physical custody of the children. Their work is doubled. Their emotional demands are more than doubled because of all of the relational chaos in the parent's life as well as the lives of the children.

However, some parents are functioning much like a single parent because the other parent is not invested into the children's lives, even though the entire family still lives in the same house. This causes conflict. Research shows that conflict in the family is the most consistent characteristic of children who have academic problems, problems with siblings, and problems with peers.[1] Therefore, it is imperative that you do your part to ensure that the kids have the environment they need.

In Chapter 5, I highlighted the 12.2 hours of unpaid household work that ladies do above those hours of men. In order for your wife to not feel abandoned, you must also actively participate in the raising of your children. The absent father does not have to live in a different house to have the same negative impact on a child as the father who abandoned his children. In fact, it has been my experience that children who have been abandoned have a tendency to idolize the absent parent because they want to assume that the absent parent loves them and has a reasonable excuse for the absence. Therefore, a parent, who still lives in the home, but is not involved in the children's lives, may be more difficult on a child. It is more difficult to have what you need right in front of you and you never get to enjoy that need being met.

As important as your spouse's needs are, you must also take responsibility for the needs of your children because you children need their dad. Let me tell you a story to illustrate this point:

One month before I turned 13 years old, my family moved to Kennedy Home in Kinston, NC. My dad accepted a job as the new director of this group home for children. We had not been there very long, and I was a part of a group of guys that were picking teams to play basketball. We all agreed that one team would wear shirts, and the other team would be "skins." One guy in particular, who was approximately my age, was working very hard to be on the shirts team. I tried to reassure him by making a comment, which I now consider to have been very inappropriate. I said to him, "Man, nobody cares that you have a bird cage chest." He looked at me very directly, and said, "It is not my chest." I just left it alone at that point.

After the game, he decided to show me the reason he did not want to take off his shirt. On his back, he had very large burn scars. His skin was raised where the burn welts used to be. He shared with me that he was "talking back" to his dad as dad was about to finish frying some chicken. As a punishment, dad took the chicken out of the grease, and threw this boiling grease on my friend's back. Of course, the Department of Social Services removed my friend from his dad's care because of this incident.

My friend did not get on the school bus the following morning. I began to ask about him, and some of my other friends told me that he ran away in the middle of the night so he could get back to his "home with dad." That day, I learned that every child's biological parents are special to that child, and the vast majority of children will forgive almost anything in exchange for the hope of being loved by their parent. Unfortunately, my friend passed away, and never had the relationship with his dad that he desired.

If you are a parent, there is not a substitute for you. Step-parents can have very special and positive relationships with children; but it is different, and those relationships need to be valued, based on the real characteristics of that relationship. Step-parents should not try to replace the biological parent. Again, there is not a substitute. *Sharing the responsibility of raising your children with your spouse, or your children's mother is romantic.* Even if you do not want to be in relationship with your children's mother, the greatest thing you can do for your children is overcome any obstacle that is in the way of you actively participating in your child or children's life.

Prayer: *LORD, You are my heavenly Father. You are always there, and always provide loving discipline and guidance. Help me to follow your example, and be the best father I can be. Amen.*

Chapter 23

Lovingly Discipline Your Children

Did you grow up hearing "Spare the rod and spoil the child"? The well-known phrase, is often used to "biblically" justify physical punishment or spankings of children. For many, this has included spankings with a switch, paddle, or other representative of the "rod." Many people believe this statement is from the Bible, and will point to Proverbs 13:24. Yet, carefully reading this verse communicates a different meaning. This exact phrase is not in the Bible, and the above-mentioned verse does not affirm physical punishment as discipline.

Here is the actual verse from Proverbs 13:24 (*The New International Version*): "Whoever spares the rod hates their children, but the one who loves their children is careful to discipline them."[1] Even when you look at the verse in the original Hebrew, there is not a word in the verse that can be translated "spoils."[2] The verse does not say anything about a child's reaction to discipline or the lack of it. It is all about discipline being a requirement of love.

So, what does "the rod" represent? During biblical times, shepherds generally carried two tools with them: a rod and a staff. In fact, these tools are highlighted in the 23rd Psalm: "Your rod and your staff, they protect and comfort me."[3] How would you get protection and comfort from a rod or staff if it is used to hit you? The rod was a club, which was about four feet in length, and the shepherds used them to defeat wild animals that attacked the sheep, or people who were trying to steal a sheep.

In the Old Testament, there is a story which illustrates this point. David was a young teenager, and his father asked him to leave his flock of sheep to carry some grain and bread to his adult brothers who were fighting the Philistines. The Philistines had issued a challenge for one man from each side would fight "to the death"; whichever side won would enslave the other side. The Philistines had Goliath, who was a giant and a champion warrior. All of the men of Israel were afraid. When David told King Saul that he would fight Goliath, he referenced two animals, a lion and a bear, that he caught attacking a sheep. David indicated that he chased down the lion and the bear and "struck it".[4] It appears he used a rod to do just that. Therefore, the rod is not symbolic of hitting the child. It is symbolic of protecting the child from danger.

The staff is a long stick, one end of which shepherds would often place in water. Over a period of days, the shepherd will gradually bend the end of it into the shepherd's crook. It is used to hold the sheep for sheering or to guide them in the direction that the shepherd desires. If a sheep started to go in the wrong direction, the shepherd could put the crook around the sheep's neck and guide it back into the flock.[5]

When you discipline your children or teens, take a moment to think about your interactions with them before you just "teach them a lesson." Rarely do we need to defend a child from an attacking bear or lion. Yet, the dangers of our hyper-sexual, drug infested, and overall permissive society are everywhere. How are you using your *proverbial rod* to defend children and teens from the dangers in our world? Do you use your *proverbial shepherd's crook* to guide them back in the way that they should go?

The purpose of this chapter is not to indicate that it is never appropriate to use physical punishment or spankings. It is to indicate that Proverbs 13:24 should not be used as proof that spankings are the required first step to "train a child in the way she or he should go." As a parent or a person in a different role that has disciplinary responsibility with a child, remember that your first responsibilities must be to protect and guide him lovingly. Use your own creativity to explore ways to accomplish these goals without making a physical assault your first choice. As the Word of God actually states, carefully discipline or guide your children as an act of love. *Lovingly disciplining your children is romantic.*

Prayer: LORD, *Help me to love my children and/or step-children in a way that will resemble you as my Good Shepherd. Amen.*

Chapter 24

Don't Kiss and Tell

We live in a very highly sexualized society. The entertainment industry requires that actresses meet such incredibly unrealistic standards. To meet those standards, some will have surgery so that bags of saline can be put in their body in order to create the illusion of feminine perfection. Then some will utilize social media as a platform on which they can openly share sexualized images of themselves in order to gain attention and then capitalize on the popularity that is gained. A few have gone so far as to "accidently" release video of themselves in actual sex acts. This type of screaming for attention in hopes that the attention will vault the individual into fame and fortune has negatively impacted our society. By saying that, I am not just blaming the actresses. Because men respond to it, the actresses and the entertainment industry, as a whole, continue to use it. This encourages a culture where sex is no longer a private affair.

I am not trying to suggest that we should go back to the days when sexuality was an unspoken topic. However, talking about sex without a reason that honors your marriage is disrespectful to your spouse. Do you tell highly sexualized jokes to other guys? Would you tell the same joke if your wife was with you? Would you tell the same joke if you had to phrase it in a way that the sexualized lady in the joke was your wife, your sister, or your mother?

Imagine yourself sitting in the mall as you wait for your wife to finish in the restroom. You notice a very attractive lady. You watch every move of that lady's walk as your neck turns from the far left to the far right. You do not notice that your wife has walked up behind you and she observes your gawking, and just wonders about your thoughts. If you are trying to look at the world "through her eyes," what do you anticipate that she feels in that scenario? Jesus said, "But I tell you that anyone who looks at a woman lustfully has already committed adultery with her in his heart".[1] This can't make her happy that she invested her entire life into you. Think about the brief excitement that you feel when looking at that woman you don't even know, and then compare that to the level of investment your wife has made into you. If you do a cost-benefit analysis of this situation, it simply does not make sense to sinfully look at a woman and simultaneously create feelings of doubt, insecurity, being unacceptable, unworthy, and plainly "not pretty enough" in your spouse.

Here is the truth: Proverbs 5:19 affirms your wife as "a loving doe, a graceful deer – may her breast satisfy you always, may you always be intoxicated with her love."[2] If you choose to always be focused on her, and you choose to romance her in the ways she desires, and you choose to work with her as you invest your life into her as she has invested her life in you, then you will not need any other breasts.

Faithfulness, in all ways, is romantic. Your wife deserves for you to treat her and the sexual aspect of your relationship with the utmost respect, honor, and appropriate confidentiality. Your friends do not need to know what does or does not happen in your bedroom, unless you are talking to someone that will provide helpful encouragement, and you have your wife's permission to share.

Prayer: LORD, *help me, as a man, to honor my wife as a beautiful woman, and see her in the way that you see her. When we are intimate, help me to understand that my goal must be to personally connect with her. With the exception of a trusted pastor, counselor, or mutually-agreed upon friend, help us to only share our intimacy with you. Amen.*

Chapter 25

Have A Good Fight!

Most people do not think of fighting as romantic. When people do not treat each other with respect during a conflict, married life can be horrible. Yet, conflict in marriage is inevitable, and conflict will either bring you closer together or slowly tear you apart. Take a moment to think about that. Conflict will either bring you closer together, or slowly tear you apart. Your attitude is often what makes the difference. To predictably have a "good fight," you must take some proactive steps that will help ensure that your conflict will bring you closer together. A good fight occurs when family members remain loving and respectful during the conversation so that they are able to work together as a team to solve the problem. The alternative is to use the problem as an excuse to verbally attack a family member.

Imagine a group of middle school boys who are playing a pickup game of baseball. Inevitably, there will be some level of conflict because the boys will be arguing about who is on which team, the rules of the game, or who is safe and who is out. If an adult comes along with a bunch of t-shirts for the boys, that have a team logo on the front, and an individualized number on the back, the arguments lose intensity. The boys begin to work together to prepare for the upcoming double-header against their newest rival. When you argue with your wife, do you have a team mindset or do you focus on winning, even if you have to bend the rules or be disrespectful? Do you work with your wife to solve the problem that is invading the intimacy between you?

God has designed our brains to always focus on protecting ourselves. When human beings are threatened, we will involuntarily look for a way out. If that does not work, we plan on how we can fight our way through the threat. This process is commonly referred to as "fight or flight." The more threatened a person feels, the more focused on one of these two options she or he becomes. If a person has a loaded gun in your face, you will not be worried about the butterfly that is nearby. You will focus on getting away or taking away the gun. These involuntary neurological processes also function when a person is being verbally assaulted. If someone is yelling and screaming at you, do you feel the need to defend yourself? Most people will defend themselves by retaliating with the same type of behavior regardless of the merits of their concern. No one enjoys being assaulted . . . physically or verbally. Therefore, your state of mind prior to and during the argument really matters.

The first step to being ready for a good fight is to *crucify yourself*. The natural state of humanity is to always want your own way. Yet, Romans 6:6 tells us, "For we know that our old self was crucified with him so that the body of sin might be done away with, that we should no longer be slaves to sin."[1] It is not that you should never get what you want, but you should have an attitude that is open to all possibilities. The only way to do that is to crucify yourself with Christ and yet live.

Honor your commitment is step two. The traditional wedding vows are based on a promise in the book of Ruth. "But Ruth said, 'Do not urge me to leave you or to return from following you. For where you go I will go, and where you lodge I will lodge. Your people shall be my people, and your God my God. Where you die I will die, and there will I be buried. May the Lord do so to me and more also if anything but death parts me from you.' "[2] Maybe these are the words you said as your wedding vows. Maybe you wrote your own wedding vows. Regardless of the words in your wedding ceremony, you made a commitment before God and the witnesses who attended your wedding. Therefore, before you have an argument, think about your commitment, and reaffirm it to yourself.

Step three is *resist temptations*. Verbally assaulting someone, using hurtful words, and using the silent treatment are examples of temptations that will impair your ability to have a good fight. 1 Cor. 10:13 tells us, "No temptation has seized you except what is common to man, and God is faithful; he will not let you be tempted beyond what you can bear. But, when you are tempted, he will always provide a way out so that you can stand up under it".[3] God will help you avoid these if you have already crucified yourself and are open to God's guidance and direction in your life.

Step four involves *investigating God's way* or the practical application of God's Word. Jesus said, "But seek first his kingdom and his righteousness and all these things will be given to you as well".[4] Notice that you are investigating God's Word before you even talk with your spouse or other family member. You may need to talk to someone that can help you find the practical application for your particular problem.

Step five is *submit to servant-leadership*. For many people the word "submit," which is found in Ephesians 5:22, is a struggle. "Wives submit to your husbands as to the Lord"[5] whereas husbands are told to "Love your wives just as Christ loved the Church and gave himself up for her"[6]. Many times conflicts are a power struggle. Remember that your wife is your marital partner of equal value. It is not her job to be anyone's doormat. Rather, partner with your spouse with an attitude that allows you to work together to solve the problem that is invading the intimacy of your relationship.

Step six is to *talk to each other*. Eph. 4:15 states, "Instead, speaking the truth in love, we will in all things grow up into him who is the Head, that is, Christ".[7] You are now ready to have the conversation that will involve respect for each other. When you successfully solve the problem, you will be closer to each other and the conflict will not have torn you apart. An additional benefit to this renewed closeness is that you will have even more confidence in your ability to problem solve together the next time.

You might be wondering how you can remember all of that. Notice the first letter of each phrase.

Crucify yourself
Honor your commitment
Resist temptations
Investigate God's way
Submit to servant-leadership
Talk to each other.

Conflict is inevitable in families. However, if you take just a few seconds to think through the acrostic, and apply them to your attitude about the conflict, then you will most likely have a respectful and good fight. *Having a good fight is romantic.* If you work together as a team to expel the problem that has invaded the intimacy between you, you will be successful. As a married couple, your actions will teach your children how to have conflict. If your example is a good one, they will most often choose the behaviors that you model. If your example is not so good, they will do likewise. It will, once again, either bring you closer or tear you apart.

Prayer: LORD, Help me to remember, even when I am angry or otherwise upset, that it is not all about me. You have ordained our marriage, and it is my job to do everything I can to maintain peace and love through the conflict in our home. Amen.

Chapter 26

What If Destructive Conflict Erupts?

Generally, there is not anything productive that comes out of destructive conflict. Once it starts, the best thing to do is just stop the conversation. Here is an idea that may help you in that process.

Initiate a conversation with your wife and explain that you want a way for both of you to stop a destructive conflict. Ask your wife to identify her most favorite date she has ever shared with you. You identify the same. Then, discuss your choices and the reasons for your choices. See if you can mutually agree on a favorite date where you enjoyed a particularly close and intimate conversation. Maybe this date is when you first really considered your relationship as serious and you were so focused on everything positive. You might choose the moment you proposed and she said "Yes!" Now, think of a word or phrase that is a unique reminder of your mutually chosen special occasion. Good examples might include the food you ate on the date, the name of the location where you met, or the name of a movie that made both of you laugh aloud.

Once you have your mutually agreed upon phrase, make an agreement together that the phrase will be the code word to announce that one of you believes the conversation is becoming destructive and unproductive. Imagine you are in the middle of an argument, and your wife suddenly said "Lasagna and garlic bread," or whatever phrase you chose. The phrase is so out of context for the conversation, that its identification is undeniable. Often times, couples will start to laugh. The second part of your agreement is that you will simply walk away from each other once your phrase is called. If one of you is feeling that the conversation is destructive and unproductive, there will most likely not be anything positive to result. Therefore, the best thing you can do is to walk away from each other.

The third part of this agreement is that you both use the code word or phrase as a reminder of a very positive experience you shared. Let this reminder help you to refocus on the fact that you are partners and you can't hurt the other person without also hurting yourself. An additional word of caution is this: If your spouse calls your phrase, this is an indication that she is feeling in some way threatened. This is not the time to get in the last word or deny that you are behaving in a way that she should perceive as threatening. Just respect her boundaries and walk away.

Respectfully walking away will honor your wife, and children. However, this phrase is not a way to avoid a problem. Once a few minutes have passed, the person who called your particular code word or phrase has the responsibility to re-initiate the conversation by asking the other party of she or he is ready to resume the conversation with a goal of making it productive and respectful. If the person who did not call the code word or phrase is not ready, then she or he can call it again. This method can go back and forth as often as necessary because the goal is to have a good fight. Review the CHRIST model of a good fight that I shared in chapter 27. Then, try again. *Proactively applying these steps to stop a destructive and unproductive fight is romantic because it proves to your wife that you are more interested in resolving conflict with her in a way that honors her needs than you are defeating her.* Defeating your wife in a fight is never really a win. It is a failure of your leadership, and evidence that you prefer to feel superior while requiring your children to live in your war zone as opposed to loving your wife through all conflict. If you and your wife can't see your way to do that together, seek help from a pastoral counselor, licensed marriage and family therapist, or other mental health professional. It is impossible for your wife to feel loved, honored, and cherished while you are yelling at her.

Prayer: LORD, help me to recognize that productive conflict is the pathway to peace. I need confidence in my ability to embrace productive conflict, as well as my ability to identify and stop destructive conflict. Amen.

Chapter 27

Coupon Ring

In the introduction, I highlighted that most ladies do not think that anything is romantic if they must ask for what they want or tell their husband what to do. In Chapter 2, I explained that romance is the evidence that love for her is still in your heart. That is why your creativity must be accessed so it really does come from your heart. However, their romantic needs that you don't think about, are also important. So, how can a lady have an opportunity to ask for something that he has already agreed to do? A coupon ring is an idea that can overcome this difficult issue.

A coupon ring is something that you can make for her which indicates all kinds of different ideas that you are willing to do whenever she expresses the need by giving you a coupon. You can follow these simple instructions to make her a coupon book:

Go to Staples, or some other office supply store, and purchase the following items (if you don't already have them):
1 package of multicolored 3 x 5 index cards ($5.99)
A small box of 2-inch loose-leaf rings ($4.09)
A one-hole punch. ($1.79)[1]

Below is a copy of the letter I wrote to my wife when I did this. It explains the process to make the coupon ring. Feel free to use it and adapt it to your unique situation.

Cheryl,

As a therapist, one of the things I have learned about most women is they want their man to be so observant and aware of their needs, that the lady does not even have to ask for the needs to be met. As we have discussed, this is true for you as well because you said that my awareness of your needs indicates that I am paying attention and value your needs being met. To you, my focus on your needs is an expression of my love. In my office, many ladies have said, "If I have to ask for it, it does not mean anything anymore."

Men on the other hand, sometimes including me, have "the squeaky wheel gets the grease type of attitude" in relationships. We expect ladies to tell us what they need. If we don't hear anything, we assume everything is ok. Many men are willing to do anything they are asked to do, but just do not understand the need women have for their man to just do it. This creates a struggle: The man is willing but does not know what to do, and the woman wants him to do something, but she feels that the romance is lost if she must ask.

My solution to this quandary is a coupon ring, and your first one is in this box. You will receive a new coupon ring at least each Christmas. However, if you need more coupons, I will gladly make you a new one. This coupon ring is designed to "courageously" express my willingness and desire to meet all of your needs, and as many of your wants as I can. However, sometimes I just don't know when you have a need, what that need is, and how I can best make that happen. Therefore, when you have a need, and I am not recognizing the need, these coupons represent my willingness to meet your need at any time. No matter what I am doing, if you present me a coupon, I will stop and meet that need immediately, or if the need is something that requires planning and thought, we will immediately discuss how we will work together to ensure that need or want is met.

You will notice that the coupons are different colors. These colors represent different categories. The white cards are coupons for everyday items that you will never over use or exhaust. You do not even need to present the coupons for these. For example, there is a coupon for a hug that last as long as you desire. That card represents my willingness and desire to give you a hug any and every time you want one. I will hold you until your need is met.

The blue cards are the *chores cards*. For example, there are cards that involve cooking dinner, cleaning the bathrooms, doing maintenance to your car, and many other items. We will always share household chores and tasks, but sometimes you may be in a situation where you just need a break. Yet, the needs of the household must be addressed. It is my desire that you know you can always come to me and I will help you complete a task, or just do it while you rest or attend to another issue.

The yellow cards are *quality family time cards*. These cards are designed for you to be able to plan a family activity and expect that I will be present and ready to participate. You also could use these cards to ask me to plan a family activity and surprise you, or ask me to join you in planning a family activity. Examples could be a family cook out, a day trip to the beach, or a birthday party for one of the kids. I enjoy spending time with our family, and I look forward to many of these activities in the future.

The orange cards are for *travel*. Here we will list places that we would like to go and any details that we want about the trip. I have started us with a list of a few national parks, a trip to the mountains of NC during peak season for the leaves changing, and a special trip that I will plan when we return to our honeymoon cabin. I look forward to see what trips you will add.

The purple cards are *just for us*, including pure romance. There will be times that you need and want my undivided attention. We will also need times for us to do special things together. For example, I am sure you will find multiple coupons for dinner for two at Chico's. There are cards here for us to take a walk together and just enjoy each other's company. There are cards for you to have a back massage. There are also some cards for a variety of physical intimacies.☺

I have written coupons for many of the good ideas that I have. I have included some blank cards so you can write your own coupons in each of the categories. Also, it is important that you pay attention to your coupon ring because you never know when I might slip a new one in and hope that you find it. We can write coupons for things we would like to do in the future. It will be like a bucket list, and a place to record ideas of things we want to do again. I hope you can accept this gift as evidence that I never want your needs or wants to go un-noticed or unmet. I hope you will playfully have fun with this, and my gift will be something special throughout the year. I want you to write your own coupons and realize that I am committed to creating the environment that you need so you can grow and become all that God created you to be.

I love you,

David

Once you have the above-mentioned items and have written out your own coupons, just punch a hole in the top left corner and place them on the ring. As you can see, this gives your wife the opportunity to select an activity that she would like, and she doesn't have to initiate the activity because you already initiated it. *Coupon rings are romantic.*

Prayer: *LORD, help me to pay attention to the subtle ways that my wife communicates her wants, needs, and desires to me. Help me to know how to respond in ways that are a match for her. Help her to know that my attention to the details in her life is an expression of my love for her. Amen.*

PART 3: CONCLUSIONS

Chapter 28

Putting It All Together

You have made it to the last chapter. For some of you, this may have been the first book you have actually read in a long time. Others of you, I am sure, have skipped to the last chapter to see if you can get the gist of it without reading the whole book. I am going to try to help you out with that, and also hope that I can inspire you to actually go back and read the rest of the book.

The message of this book is simple: Romance after the wedding is not the same as before you said "I do." To be romantic now, you must see the world through her eyes, or through her perspective of the world. She chose to invest her life into you, and now she needs more than an annual box of chocolates as a return on her investment. Seeing the world through her eyes will help you recognize the things that she needs in her environment in order to grow and become all God created her to be.

My own definition of romance is this: Using your own creativity to express the love that is in your heart in ways that make your wife feel loved, honored, and cherished. Your wife can't tell you how to show your own creativity because she is not looking for the action as much as she is looking for the evidence that the action reveals. If you choose to express love by completing a task, giving her your undivided attention, giving her a card that expresses your thoughts, sharing a compliment, or by touching her physically in a way that she appreciates,[1] she can experience romantic love that is coming from your heart, and not from a place where you only gave because she asked for it. Romantic expressions that your wife has to ask for just do not count to her. Men often enjoy the chase of a dating relationship and feel that the chase is over after the nuptials. Nothing could be further from the truth. However, the process of the chase changes. It is not that your wife needs constant reassurance. Your wife needs to experience your love on a regular basis and not have to rely on what you said before the wedding.

I have provided you 23 practical ideas on how to do this, and my hope is you will take these ideas, apply your own creativity to them, and develop your own style of marital romance. Remember: Your wife is your fruitful vine. If you want her to continue to produce fruit, you must ensure that she has the right environment in which she can grow. You are a major part of that environment, and you must choose to actively participate in its creation. You can't just continue on auto-pilot or act like your dad did with your mom. Your wife's romantic needs may be very different from the romantic needs of your mom.

Some of you might think that this whole romantic thing is hard. . . maybe too hard. Since I am a minister and a therapist, I often have couples come into my office who want counseling from a biblical perspective. Some of those couples have power struggles and these struggles are often based around the fifth chapter of Ephesians.

The Apostle Paul was writing to the church he had previously planted in Ephesus. He wrote, "Wives submit yourselves to your own husbands as you do to the Lord. For the husband is the head of the wife as Christ is the head of the Church, his body, of which he is the Savior."[2] However, husbands are directed to "love your wives, just as Christ loved the church and gave himself up for her."[3] We are going to focus on the role of the husband, and not the wife. If you are responding to your wife by loving her only when you see evidence of her submission to you, these next paragraphs are for you. Take your Bible and flip a few pages to the right from Ephesians 5 and find Philippians 2:1-11:

> "Therefore if you have any encouragement from being united with Christ, if any comfort from his love, if any common sharing in the Spirit, if any tenderness and compassion, [2] then make my joy complete by being like-minded, having the same love, being one in spirit and of one mind. [3] Do nothing out of selfish ambition or vain conceit. Rather, in humility value others above yourselves, [4] not looking to your own interests but each of you to the interests of the others.
> [5] In your relationships with one another, have the same mindset as Christ Jesus:

6 Who, being in very nature[a] God,
    did not consider equality with God something to be used to his
own advantage;
7 rather, he made himself nothing
    by taking the very nature[b] of a servant,
    being made in human likeness.
8 And being found in appearance as a man,
    he humbled himself
    by becoming obedient to death—
        even death on a cross!
9 Therefore God exalted him to the highest place
    and gave him the name that is above every name,
10 that at the name of Jesus every knee should bow,
    in heaven and on earth and under the earth,
11 and every tongue acknowledge that Jesus Christ is Lord, to the
glory of God the Father."[4]

If we as husbands are to love our wives as Christ loved the church, then Paul's description of Jesus in Phil. 2: 1-11 is our instruction manual! Your position as the "head of the house" is not something you should ever use to throw your weight around (proverbially) in order to get your way. As "the head," your job is to be the servant. As a servant, you lead in the same way that Jesus led. . . by thinking of the needs of others first, and that includes your wife's needs for romance.

Choosing to do these things may not be your idea of a "fun time" right now. Jesus was obedient to the point of death. You must at least be obedient to the point romance. Maybe your marriage has lost the "loving feelings." If so, I would guess that a significant part of that struggle is because you have not been meeting your wife's need for romance. Remember: "It is better to live on a corner of the roof than share a house with a quarrelsome woman."[5] Do the things that she needs and her reactions will eventually produce the fruit you need and help you to enjoy the actions of romance.

So, it is now time for you to take some action. Rather than seeing yourself as the "head of the house," think of yourself as the servant of the house.

Jesus looked at our situation of sin, discovered what we needed, and provided the solution. Look at your wife, and discover what she needs. She needs real romance that includes the obvious evidence that your heart is still fully invested into her. She must see that you want to create the environment in which she can grow and become all that God designed her to be. Determine her love language, and start speaking that language. If you don't enjoy speaking that language, you must remember that it is *not* all about you. I am not trying to suggest that you should not enjoy your marriage. I am saying that you may need to do some things that are not a priority because they are your wife's priorities. If you will do this, it is my sincere belief that your fruit-producing wife will provide you so much joy, that doing the things she wants will become something to which you look forward. Real romance is not sitting around with tissues looking at the latest Hallmark Channel movie, or something that makes you feel like you are no longer "a man's man." It is the expression of the love from your heart in creative ways which allow your wife to continue to be glad she said "I do."

Prayer: *LORD, help me to learn my wife's love language and speak it on a daily basis. Help me to be attentive to the things she has to say that will point me toward romantic opportunities. Help me be obedient to the point of romance. Amen.*

Epilogue

Let's continue the conversation: My email address is davidmorrowlmft@gmail.com. My blog is www.romancingyourwife.com, and I invite you to subscribe to the blog. I will continue to post thoughts and ideas there, and also ask you to interact with me and other men who are trying to be the best husband they can be. Send me an email with your thoughts and feedback about what I have written. Send me an email that details how you have applied the information in this book and the results. If you do something that your wife considers romantic and very positive, ask her to send me an email that details your actions and the feelings she experienced as a result. I will post the emails, which are appropriate, on the blog and we all can learn and gain ideas from each other. As the conclusion highlights, it is time to take action with a goal of creatively communicating to your wife that she is still loved, honored, and cherished. If we can learn from each other, we will all be more successful and our wives will enjoy producing fruit that is designed just for us.

References

Introduction:
[1] Conver, L., Ph.D. (1995, August 31). *The Psychology and Theology of Family Relationships*. Lecture presented in Southern Baptist Theological Seminary, Louisville, KY.
[2] Bible: Matthew 23:27 NLT

Chapter 1: Defining Romance
None

Chapter 2: So, How Do I Do It?
[1] Ardolino, E. (Director), & Bergstein, E. (Writer). (1987). *Dirty Dancing* [Video file]. United States: Great American Films Limited Partnership.

Chapter 3: Spiritually Motivating Your Creativity
[1] Conver, L., Ph.D. (1995, August 31). *The Psychology and Theology of Family Relationships*. Lecture presented in Southern Baptist Theological Seminary, Louisville, KY.
[2] Bible: Psalms 128 NLT

Chapter 4: Identifying the Needs of Her Environment
[1] Chapman, G., Ph.D. (2015). *The Five Love Languages: The Secret to Love That Lasts*. Chicago, IL: Northfield Publishing. P. 14
[2] Chapman, G., Ph.D. (2015). *The Five Love Languages: The Secret to Love That Lasts*. Chicago, IL: Northfield Publishing. P.15
[3] Zig Ziglar. (n.d.). BrainyQuote.com. Retrieved February 23, 2017, from BrainyQuote.com Web site:
https://www.brainyquote.com/quotes/quotes/z/zigziglar617761.html

Chapter 5: Sweep Her Off Her Feet
[1] Time spent working by full- and part-time status, gender, and location in 2014 : The Economics Daily. (n.d.). Retrieved July 9, 2016, from http://www.bls.gov/opub/ted/2015/time-spent-working-by-full-and-part-time-status-gender-and-location-in-2014.htm

[2] Leman, K. (2006). *Sex begins in the kitchen: creating intimacy to make your marriage sizzle.* Grand Rapids, MI: Revell. P. 9-10.

Chapter 6: Money: Power House or Power Struggle
[1] Hawks, H. (Director). (1953). *Gentleman Prefer Blondes* [Video file]. United States: 20th Centry Fox.
[2] Billy Graham. (n.d.). BrainyQuote.com. Retrieved March 2, 2017, from BrainyQuote.com Web site:
https://www.brainyquote.com/quotes/quotes/b/billygraha626354.html

Chapter 7: Loyalty
[1] T.D. Jakes Show on Twitter. (n.d.). Retrieved September 19, 2016, from http://t.co/cV6ATETM8J

Chapter 8: Is Her Body Mine?
[1] Bible: 1st Corinthians 7:3-4 NLT
[2] Padfield, D. (n.d.). Corinth, Greece | Temples of Aphrodite, Apollo, Poseidon, Asklepios, Hygieia. Retrieved August 5, 2016, from http://www.biblelandhistory.com/greece/corinth.html
[3] Perrottet, T. (n.d.). Ancient Greek Temples of Sex. Retrieved August 5, 2016, from http://thesmartset.com/article11210701/
[4] Barclay, W. (1956). *The Daily Study Bible Series: the Letters to Timothy, Titus, and Philemon.* Philadelphia, PA: Westminster. P. 34

Chapter 9: Manage Your Emotions
None

Chapter 10: Supporting Her Hopes and Dreams
[1] (2011, October 25). Retrieved September 02, 2017, from https://vimeo.com/31077792
[2] Gaither, B., & Abraham, K. (2003). *It's More Than Music: Life Lessons on Friends, Faith, and What Matters Most.* WarnerFaith.

[3] Bill Gaither (gospel singer). (2017, February 22). Retrieved September 10, 2016, from https://en.wikipedia.org/wiki/Bill_Gaither_(gospel_singer)

Chapter 11: Quality Time
[1] Ziglar, Z. (1985). *Steps to the Top*. Gretna, LA: Pelican Publishing Company. P. 55
[2] Chapman, G., Ph.D. (2015). *The Five Love Languages: The Secret to Love That Lasts*. Chicago, IL: Northfield Publishing.

Chapter 12: The Little Things
[1] DaleCarnegie.org. (n.d.). Retrieved September 10, 2016, from http://dalecarnegie.org/
[2] Carnegie, D. (1998). *Dale Carnegie's lifetime plan for success: How to win friends & influence people ; How to stop worrying & start living*. New York: Galahad Books. P. 52.
[3] Carnegie, D. (1936). *How To Win Friends And Influence People*. New York, NY: Simon and Schuster. P. 287

Chapter 13: Date Night
None

Chapter 14: Unexpected Surprises
[1] Corona, V. (n.d.). Retrieved December 23, 2016, from http://quoteinvestigator.com/2013/12/17/breaths/

Chapter 15: Met Needs Without Prompting
None

Chapter 16: Decision Making
None

Chapter 17: Show Her Your Strength
[1] Bible: 1st Corinthians 10:13 NLT
[2] Jenkins, C (2016, November 7) Personal Interview.

[3] A quote by Franklin D. Roosevelt. (n.d.). Retrieved September 05, 2016, from http://www.goodreads.com/quotes/172689-courage-is-not-the-absence-of-fear-but-rather-the

[4] Serenity Prayer. (2017, February 17). Retrieved October 3, 2016, from https://en.wikipedia.org/wiki/Serenity_Prayer

Chapter 18: Show Her Your Weakness
None

Chapter 19: Honesty
[1] Yang, S. (2014, July 01). 5 Years Ago Bernie Madoff Was Sentenced to 150 Years In Prison – Here's How His Scheme Worked. Retrieved October 06, 2016, from http://www.businessinsider.com/how-bernie-madoffs-ponzi-scheme-worked-2014-7
[2] Bernard L. Madoff Investment Securities LLC Liquidation Proceeding. (n.d.). Retrieved March 06, 2017, from http://www.madofftrustee.com/
[3] Bible: Proverbs 12:22 NLT

Chapter 20: Develop a Spiritual Discipline
[1] Bible: Philippians 1:20 NLT
[2] Barclay, W. (1956). *The Daily Study Bible Series: the Letters to the Philippians, Colossians, and Thessalonians.* Philadelphia, PA: Westminster.
[3] Bible: Philippians 3:8 NIV

Chapter 21: Thoughtful Gifts
[1] Chapman, G., Ph.D. (n.d.). Receiving Gifts. Retrieved November 09, 2016, from http://www.5lovelanguages.com/languages/receiving-gifts/

Chapter 22: Love Your Wife By Leading Your Children
[1] Children of Single Mothers: How Do They Really Fare? (n.d.). Retrieved September 15, 2016, from https://www.psychologytoday.com/blog/living-single/200901/children-single-mothers-how-do-they-really-fare

Chapter 23: Lovingly Discipline Your Children

[1] Bible: Proverbs 13:24 NIV

[2] Proverbs 13:24 Hebrew Text Analysis. (n.d.). Retrieved October 09, 2016, from http://biblehub.com/text/proverbs/13-24.htm

[3] Bible: Psalm 23:4 NLT

[4] Bible: 1 Sam. 17:35 NIV

[5] Function of Shepherd's Staff (Forerunner Commentary). (n.d.). Retrieved November 09, 2016, from http://www.bibletools.org/index.cfm/fuseaction/Topical.show/RTD/CGG/ID/14585/Function-Shepherds-Staff.htm

Chapter 24: Don't Kiss and Tell

[1] Bible: Matthew 5:28 NIV

[2] Bible: Proverbs 5:19 NIV

Chapter 25: Have a Good Fight!

[1] Bible: Romans 6:6 NIV

[2] Bible: Ruth 1:16-17 NIV

[3] Bible: 1 Corinthians 10:13 NIV

[4] Bible: Matthew 6:33 NIV

[5] Bible: Ephesians 5:22 NIV

[6] Bible: Ephesians 5:22 NIV

[7] Bible: Ephesians 4:15 NIV

Chapter 26:
None

Chapter 27: Coupon Ring

[1] Office Supplies, Printer Ink, Toner, Computers, Printers & Office Furniture | Staples®. (n.d.). Retrieved November 09, 2016, from http://www.staples.com/

Chapter 28: Putting It All Together

[1] Chapman, G., Ph.D. (n.d.). Discover Your Love Language. Retrieved December 12, 2016, from http://www.5lovelanguages.com/

[2] Bible: Ephesians 5:22-23 NIV

[3] Bible: Ephesians 5:26 NIV

[4] Bible: Philippians 2:1-11 NIV

[5] Bible: Proverbs 21:9 NIV

About the Author

David Morrow is an ordained minister and a licensed marriage and family therapist who has been working in the mental health field since July of 1990. He is a graduate from Campbell University in Buies Creek, NC, and from Southern Seminary in Louisville, KY. At Campbell University, David majored in religion, and at Southern Seminary he earned a Masters of Divinity in Pastoral Counseling. Currently, David works as a therapist at CareNet Counseling East, which is a regional office for CareNet Inc., in Greenville, NC. CareNet Inc. is a Winston Salem based state-wide ministry of pastoral counseling offices, and is also a division of the chaplaincy office of Wake Forest Baptist Health. David's professional passion is working with couples, especially couples who are blending their families, to help them achieve the type of relationship they mutually desire.

David and his wife Cheryl have developed a marriage enrichment seminar titled "Recommit, Restore, and Renew." This seminar is unique because the participants complete a short survey prior to the event so that David and Cheryl can develop a seminar that is uniquely designed to address the needs for those participants. For more information about inviting David and Cheryl to develop and present this seminar or invite David to preach in your church, contact David at davidmorrowlmft@gmail.com.

When David isn't working, he enjoys spending time with his wife and family, creating music, and playing golf with friends.

About the Photographer

Amanda Morrow, David Morrow's daughter, is a graduate from Wilmington Early College High School where she earned her high school diploma and simultaneously earned an associates degree in general studies, and a second associates degree in dramatic arts. Currently, she is a student at Appalachian State University in Boone, NC, and is double majoring in outdoor recreation and commercial photography. She is a Resident Assistant, and loves helping students transition into college life. After graduating, she plans to go to seminary and follow God's call into youth ministry. In her free time, she enjoys rock climbing, camping, and spending time with her friends.

About the Cover Photo

The setting for the cover photo is Fort Caswell on the eastern tip of Oak Island, NC. This is a special place for both Amanda and David Morrow. Fort Caswell was a federal fort that the North Carolina Baptist purchased in 1949. Since that time, the Baptist have used this site for a variety of camps and conferences. In 1980, David heard the still small voice of God here. Standing near the site of this picture, David looked to his right at the cross with the sun setting in the background. Then, he looked to his left and saw the rubble of war. At 13, David understood God present a choice. Following the way of the cross reveals God's peace. Following one's selfish desires brings the rubble of human chaos. Thirty-one years later, on the day that the cover picture was taken, Amanda accepted God's call into full-time Christian Ministry, in almost the exact same spot… Holy Ground.